The Pursuit of Salvation

The Pursuit of Salvation
A Critical Guide to the Novels of Graham Greene

Georg M. A. Gaston
Department of English
Appalachian State University
Boone, N. C.

The Whitston Publishing Company
Troy, New York
1984

CONTENTS

PREFACE

Near the end of *The Other Man,* a book-length interview published when he was approaching his eightieth birthday, Graham Greene expressed the startling thought that he was a failure. After publishing more than forty books, he still didn't think any of them were "very good," and his talent, he believed, hadn't actually reached the point of exceptional productivity. Was he perhaps asking too much of himself, or was he being too modest? No, Greene told his interviewer, he was merely being realistic. He was a "good enough writer," but he didn't belong "among the giants." Because Greene is by nature a highly controversial and paradoxical writer, his reputation will no doubt be debated by critics for many years to come. Based on my reading, however, I would say that he has certainly underestimated his achievement. When the literary history of our age is finally written, Greene is bound to figure prominently for at least two reasons. One is that his novels have led a counter-revolution against the modernist tradition which dominated fiction during the earlier part of the century. The other is that Greene has become the most eloquent voice of the anguished fears and hopes characterizing his time. It's the recognition of these factors, along with the awareness that he had established a distinctly personal world of fiction, which drew me to Greene, and eventually prompted this book.

While writing this book, I had valuable assistance and encouragement from some of my colleagues. Joseph Schwartz, the editor of *Renascence,* encouraged me to continue my research after publishing an early essay of mine on Greene. Charles Rose made several useful suggestions about how I might organize my discussion more effectively. Edwin T. Arnold helped me to smooth over certain rough spots in the manuscript. Karen Carmean was very generous in her willingness to debate the most difficult questions about Greene and then to go over the manuscript with a critical eye. For all this help, I am very grateful.

I am also thankful to the following publishers for granting

me permission to quote selected words and passages from the various books by Greene which they published. William Heinemann & Bodley Head: *The Quiet American*, 1955; *The Ministry of Fear*, 1956; *England Made Me*, 1970; *The Confidential Agent*, 1971; *Stamboul Train*, 1974; *A Burnt-Out Case*, 1974; *The End of the Affair*, 1974; *Brighton Rock*, 1975; *Our Man in Havana*, 1977; *The Power and the Glory*, 1979. Simon & Schuster: *A Sort of Life*, 1971; *The Honorary Consul*, 1973; *The Human Factor*, 1978; *Dr. Fischer of Geneva*, 1980; *Ways of Escape*, 1980; *Monsignor Quixote*, 1982. Viking-Penguin: *The Heart of the Matter*, 1948; *In Search of a Character*, 1962; *Journey Without Maps*, 1965; *The Comedians*, 1966; *Another Mexico*, 1967; *Collected Essays*, 1969; *Travels With My Aunt*, 1970.

I.
INTRODUCTION: A DIFFERENT APPROACH

Over half a century after he published his first novel in 1929, Graham Greene continues to write with vigor. And so do his critics, it would appear, since year by year the list of articles on Greene continues to grow. Yet there is something disheartening about this growing body of criticism. So much of it is inconsequential, commonplace, or simply dated.

One rather insignificant debate centers around the difference between Greene's "entertainments" and his novels. Greene himself is in large part responsible for this, at best, minor issue by having tagged some of his books with that label. When he published *Travels With My Aunt* in 1970, he finally decided to list all of his book-length fiction as novels. However, it was too late to stop the discussion.[1]

It may be true that those books which Greene used to call "entertainments" are different from his other novels, but in degree only. Basically they differ from the novels in that they are less intensely concerned with serious moral issues and deep character development than with a good story containing moral implications. These stories, because they are generally cast in the form of thrillers or farce and because they put a high premium on plot and setting, have often been successfully adapted to the idiom of the motion picture. The technique of the "entertainments," as a matter of fact, resembles that of a camera eye focusing on fast-paced action which is filled with coincidences and improbabilities. As in the case of most of the novels, the settings are usually exotic, but they are less successfully established as psychological metaphors. Taken as a whole, in fact, the art of the "entertainments" tends to be less refined than that of the novels.

Greene knew that his major accomplishments were to be found not in the "entertainments" but in his other novels. That is because, as he has confessed, he was never very ambitious in them—sometimes, it appears, writing them as preliminary studies for later works, and sometimes as forms of escape from boredom, depression, or money problems. Many times, it is true, his instincts and talent took control, and then he wrote as well in them as in his more consciously ambitious novels. Obviously, though, the "entertainments" represent Greene's minor novels.

Another debate which has had only limited value focuses on the nature of Greene the man. While much of Greene's work has yet to be fully examined, his own character has been probed and psychoanalyzed by critics perhaps more than that of any other living novelist.[2] His religious ideology in particular has been under the most intense kind of scrutiny. Yet the man and his moral convictions remain somewhat of a mystery. Is he, for example, a Pelagian, an Augustinian, a Jansenist, a Manichean, or a Christian Existentialist?[3] Such questions continue to be raised, and none of the answers so far has been fully satisfactory. Greene continues to elude any definitive labels. This is, of course, because he is a highly complex, often paradoxical, man who is writing fiction which is not confessional. He is generally writing under intense subjective pressures, but he keeps control of them through a stringent craft. The end result is a body of work in which the author remains as intriguing and remote as he is unique.

We may ultimately "know" an author through his work, but the special problem (and appeal) of Greene is that there is more than one of him. This is to say that his work has gone through several different phases. Because the critical community, by and large, has been slow to adjust to this fact, many commentaries on Greene's work now seem myopic or obsolete. As a matter of fact, much of the criticism which still retains the most excellent reputation today appears premature because it stopped with the consideration of Greene's Catholic novels.[4] Yet it's become clear with the publication of Greene's recent novels and his two autobiographical works that there is an important line of development leading from those earlier eschatological works to the more recent, highly secular ones. In a recent interview Greene himself touched on this point by proclaiming that he "always found it difficult to believe in God" and that he now called himself "a Catholic atheist."[5]

Because Greene's technique has remained more or less the same since he discovered and perfected it, and because some very astute critics have concentrated on his style, little remains to be said about this area except for structure. My intention is to address these issues, but in a subordinate way to a more significant consideration. The most obvious void that still exists, I believe, concerns questions of theme. Thus my primary effort will be directed toward an in-depth thematic exploration of all of Greene's major novels.

I believe that such an approach will bear significant results. Most important, it will reveal that throughout his career Greene has been a sophisticated romantic in pursuit of a dream worth suffering for.

II.
FINDING HIS WAY

If Greene had not written his provocative novels, he might today be known for some of the most penetrating commentary on the art of fiction.[1] His criticism is exceptional because he is willing to be unconventional, sometimes eccentric, in his literary perspectives. Ultimately trusting his intuition, he has succeeded in writing a number of essays in which he tracks down the daemon which compels some people to create fiction. Because they often arrive quickly at what Greene feels are the supreme truths about an author's art, these essays are particularly accessible to the general reader of fiction. As for the discerning readers of Greene's fiction, they will discover that these speculations are frequently self-revealing.

In this indirect fashion Greene is often his best critic. This is especially true, of course, when he is writing of those authors with whom he shares certain compulsions. Thus some of his most brilliant and self-revealing speculations are on such obsessive writers as Dickens, Mauriac, and de la Mare. But it is in his essays on Henry James that he is most obviously writing with this double vision. There, indeed, much of what he writes about James is perhaps more conspicuously true of himself than of his subject. It is certainly as true of Greene as of James that he had a "ruling fantasy which drove him to write," that this fantasy was inspired by a "sense of evil religious in its intensity," and that, believing in the supernatural, he "saw evil as an equal force with good." It is also clear that, no less than James, he had a private vision which "has left a series of novels . . . of one moral piece."[2]

Novelists may be notorious for being less than perfectly reliable when they turn their critical attention directly on their own work. But Greene writes as accurately about his own achievements as anybody.[3] He is, for instance, certainly right when he advances several lines from Browning's "Bishop Blough-ram's Apology" as an epigraph for all of his novels:

Our interest's on the dangerous edge of things.
The honest thief, the tender murder,

The supersitious artheist, demi-rep
That loves and saves her soul in new French books—

We watch while these in equilibrium keep
The giddy line midway.[4]

These lines summarize Greene's vision perfectly. The characters who populate his exotic world come readily to mind, and so does his technique of suspending them between immaterial territories.

The guiding vision of a novelist, Greene believes, is perceived by him once and for all early in his youth. In his own case, Greene first beheld his creative prospect in a number of primary dreams about amoral power. The first dream which haunted him was about "something outside that has got to come in." Later the figures of power assumed various disturbing shapes: "a troop of black skinned girls who carried poison flowers which it was death to touch; an old Arab; a half-caste; armed men with shaven heads and narrow eyes and the appearance of Tibetans out of a travel book; a Chinese detective." These adumbrate his later dreams of positive evil, represented by "the man with gold teeth and rubber surgical gloves; the old woman with ringworm; the man with his throat cut dragging himself across the carpet to the bed."[5]

These shocking dreams made the young Greene perceive evil as something frightfully real. But it was his later experience of public school which convinced him of the reality of hell. There, he remembers, he became aware of

fear and hate, a kind of lawlessness—appalling cruelties could be practiced without a second though; one met for the first time characters, adult and adolescent, who bore about them the genuine quality of evil. There was Collifax, who practiced torments with dividers; Mr. Cranden with three grim chins, a dusty gown, a kind of demoniac sensuality; from these heights evil declined towards Parlow, whose desk was filled with minute photographs—advertisements of art photos. Hell lay about them. . . .[6]

This terrifying world existed behind a door which separated the school from home and the study of the schoolmaster, who happened to be Greene's father. Because of this double life, Greene developed an anxiety about dislocation which is often expressed in his fiction. More important, the "horror and the fascination" of the school caused him to look for and to find faith. As he recalls it, he

> escaped surreptiously for an hour at a time: unknown to frontier guards, one stood on the wrong side of the border looking back—one should have been listening to Mendelssohn, but instead one heard the rabbit restlessly cropping near the croquet hoops. It was an hour of release—and also an hour of prayer. One became aware of God with an intensity. . . . And so faith came to one—shapelessly, without dogma, a presence above a croquet lawn, something associated with violence, cruelty, evil across the way. One began to believe in heaven because one believed in hell. . . .[7]

This conviction of hell on earth was re-inforced by his childhood reading. At first the works of Rider Haggard haunted him most profoundly. In fact, Haggard's exploration of the ordeal of entrapment influenced his imagination permanently. But later, when he was fourteen years old, Greene read a novel which determined his future. From the moment he picked up Marjorie Bowen's *The Viper of Milan,* he wanted to become a writer. As he remembers it:

> All the other possible futures slid away. . . . Imitation after imitation of Miss Bowen's magnificent novel went into exercise-books. . . . It was as if I had been supplied once and for all with a subject.[8]

According to Greene, Miss Bowen's novel also provided him with a creative pattern which Catholicism would later explain to him in different terms: "perfect evil walking the world where perfect good can never walk again, and only the pendulum ensures that after all in the end justice is done."[9] Greene's recollections once more bear out the facts, for evil is an omnipresent subject in his fictional world where human nature is continuously in conflict with itself and divine forces.

Greene became a Catholic when he was 22 years of age, but

it was not the ultimate turning point in his life that it might appear to be. Catholicism may have provided him with the metaphysical justification for his tormenting belief that human nature was "not black and white but black and grey."[10] Now he also became persuaded of a strange bond between hell on earth and heaven. It is, nevertheless, important to point out that his beliefs had not yet been truly challenged by an essential experience of despair.

He had courted self-destruction when he was 17 years old and imagined himself to be hopelessly in love with his sister's governess. Yet he gambled with Russian roulette not because of a conviction that life was abominable but because of a deep boredom with it at that time.[11] Out of this period of suicidal fantasies Greene emerged, as he says, "irrevocably in love with failure." He also was left with a relish for testing himself against the limits of personal endurance. This allure of the ordeal ultimately led him to take a journey to Africa when he was 31 years old, and it was then that Greene's vision achieved full maturity.[12]

While on this journey his disillusionment with what modern man had made of his childhood was confirmed. His nostalgia for the primitive, he now became convinced, was for "the finer taste, the finer pleasure, the finer terror on which one might have built." But if Greene's pessimism about his age deepened on one hand, on the other he had an experience which revived his interest in life. He had been more attracted to death than to life before. When during his journey he discovered a "passionate interest in living," however, he recalls it like a conversation.[13] Because of this new feeling for life, Greene's bleak vision of life is finally tempered by effectual love.

Since Greene writes from deep memories and fixations, the fiction he has written after his trip to Africa reflects this new faith in life. Prior to that journey his novels carry such a heavy burden of pessimism that one tends to believe only in the evil they describe. When they attempt to be affirmitive about life, they aren't very convincing and instead incline toward rather awkward melodrama. After his African experience, however, Greene's novels often succeed in capturing the true complexity of the human spectacle, consisting of suffering and betrayal but also of glory and self-sacrifice.

In a way, Greene has been writing about his spiritual journey ever since. His fictional world still retains much of its disturbing gloom. Certainly his books are still pervaded by the issues of guilt, revenge, betrayal, pursuit, and failure. Indeed, these subjects often recur with such intensity that they add up to a shattering vision of hell on earth. At such time one might be inclined to agree with the view of one critic that "a terror of what experience can do to the individual, a terror at a pre-determined corruption, is the motive force that drives Greene as a novelist."[14] Such an assessment, however, would ultimately be imprecise. Especially after his African trip, Greene began to explore the possibilities of salvation, and this search has continued in his novels in various forms for the rest of his career.

Early Novels

Greene's first published novel, *The Man Within* (1929), focuses on the character of Andrews, a young man on the run. The story, somewhat vaguely set in the early part of the 19th century, opens with the fugitive desperately making his way across the foggy Sussex Downs. He has betrayed to the law a gang of smugglers, of which he himself was a member and which was once led by his father, now by Carlyon, a man whom he has worshipped. Carlyon and three other members of the gang have escaped the authorities, and Andrews is sure they are bent on revenge and in close pursuit. At first, it might appear that he is simply running out of physical fear. However, it quickly becomes apparent that he is at the same time trying to escape his moral conscience and the haunting influence of his dead father. Thus, when he finds refuge with a courageous young woman in her cottage, he doesn't really feel safer. Instead, his panic increases because, through the woman's spiritual force, he is made to confront his tormented, divided self. What's more, he feels himself falling in love with her. As a consequence, he gives in to her suggestion that he go to the assizes held in Lewes and testify in person against the smugglers who were caught. But in Lewes, Andrews fails badly, for he not only betrays Elizabeth by giving in to the temptations of a seductive, corrupt young woman; he also proves to be so inept as a witness for the prosecution that the smugglers are freed. Now, spurred on by the fear of what the smugglers might try to do to him and the girl, who, they know, has helped him, he hurries back to Elizabeth's cottage. Finding her still safe, he declares his love, and she re-ciprocates. But the happiness of the lovers doesn't last long. Soon thereafter Elizabeth dies protecting her man from his pursuers and Andrews surrenders himself to the law as her murderer and, as a further act of atonement, appears to contemplate suicide.

Even such a brief summary of the story indicates that Greene is already dealing with many themes which would continue to fascinate him. Most obviously, there are those of betrayal, pursuit, revenge, atonement, and sacrificial love. In addition, he works in his concerns with the nature and impact of innocence, pity, responsibility, sex, childhood experiences, death, personal fragmentation, and religious belief. This is a very ambitious list of topics for any novel, much less a first one by a young writer. Eventually Greene would become a brilliant exponent of all these concerns. In this book, however, he largely fails, mainly because he has not yet discovered a way in which to mesh all the subjects together by means of an organic style and a controlling theme.

Moreover, as Greene himself came to realize, it was a book which in some ways represented a false start. In time, he would learn to write thoroughly contemporary works inspired by his own emotions and experiences. But in this novel he was obviously working under the heavy influence of several of his favorite writers, notably Robert Louis Stevenson, Henry James, Joseph Conrad, and the metaphysical poets. As a result, *The Man Within* is, as Greene says, a "very young and very sentimental" book which now seems to him "like the book of a complete stranger."[15] In other words, Greene now realizes just how overwrought, schematic, repetitive, and romantically self-indulgent it actually is. Of course, as he suggests, the underlying problem was that of youthful inexperience. He had simply not yet learned to balance in his writing certain personal and artistic elements—romanticism and realism, melodrama and irony, belief and despair.

Unfortunately, before Greene discovered what his literary path should be, he drifted through a period of misdirection. Mislead by the very encouraging reviews which *The Man Within* received,[16] and still working under the influence of other writers, especially that of Conrad, he went on to publish two books which took him even further away from the kind of novels he would eventually perfect.

The year after he published *The Man Within* he brought out *The Name of Action* (1930). This is a story which centers on a young man's entanglement in a Ruritanian revolution. The following year he published *Rumour at Nightfall* (1931). Another adventure story set in the past, it deals with the Carlist Rebellion set in Spain, a place about which Greene at that time incidentally knew next to nothing. Today it's easy to see why both of these novels were bound to be commercial and critical failures. In a manner of speaking, these highly derivative novels simply had too little of Greene himself in them. Hence it's understandable why Greene subsequently dismissed them as mere juvenilia and has decided to exclude them from the Uniform Edition of his works.

In his fourth book, *Stamboul Train* (1932),[17] Greene at last decided to try his hand at telling a story set in contemporary times. The resulting difference was nothing less than amazing. Certainly, no one could deny that there is an exciting story. One might even say that several exciting stories are recounted. In this book, Greene has gathered a number of interesting characters and put them aboard a train running from Ostend to Istanbul. During the course of the journey, we focus on the stories of a young female dancer, a Jewish merchant, a lesbian journalist, a professional criminal, and a Communist revolutionary. In addition, we meet a number of vividly drawn minor figures.[18] At first the connections between the various characters aren't very clear. But as the train continues on its way, their stories begin to intertwine, so that by the end of the trip the multiple plot takes on an impression of purposeful unity. And this impression is strengthened by the fact that Greene has by now learned a great deal about the relationship between style and subject matter.

While Greene was working on his earliest novels, he was learning some of the most valuable lessons about writing fiction from his careful study of one book in particular, Percy Lubbock's *The Craft of Fiction*. Most notably, he learned the importance of point-of-view. However, one thing that Lubbock's book couldn't teach him was actually very crucial to him. This was how to write in such a way that serious matters were carried along by a surface of physical action.

Largely because in *Stamboul Train* Greene has discovered how to convey this kind of excitement, it's his first distinctive book. At last, as he recalls, he had reached the point where, looking back at his previous efforts, he could see for himself where he had gone wrong and what he must try to do instead:

Excitement is simple: excitement is a situation, a single event. It mustn't be wrapped up in thoughts, similes, metaphors. A simile is a form of reflection, but excitement is of the moment when there is no time to reflect. Action can only be expressed by a subject, a verb and an object, perhaps a rhythm—little else. Even an adjective slows the pace or tranquilizes the nerve. . . . But I was too concerned with "the point of view" to be aware of simpler problems, to know that the sort of novel I was trying to write, unlike a poem, was not made with words but with movement, action, character. Discrimination in one's words is certainly required, but not love of one's words—that is a form of self-love, a fatal love which leads a young writer to the excesses of Charles Morgan and Lawrence Durrell, and, looking back to this period of my life, I can see that I was in danger of taking *their* road. I was only saved by failure.[19]

Because of the failure of his previous novels, Greene was in such a terrible financial plight that, for the first and only time in his life, he consciously set out to write a book which would be so popular that it might ultimately be made into a film.[20] This plan, in turn, seems to have influenced his style in a significant way. It's remarkable how cinematic his style now became. More precisely, he employs a variety of techniques usually favored by expressionistic filmmakers. Among these are superimposition, colliding images, dissolves, montage, suggestive reflections, parallel editing, tight framing, extreme angles of vision, and purposeful light and shadow. All this is done, it should be emphasized, with such skill that its cumulative effect resembles the sensual, direct impact of a great film.[21]

Mixed in with these components is one more stylistic advance which bears pointing out. This is the way Greene lays out key scenes.[22] These scenes might come at any time, but they stand out because of the import they carry. Usually, they center on Greene's primary thematic concerns, and these concerns are brought out through an exchange of dialogue. To intensify the climate of exchange, Greene tends to place two or three characters in close quarters where, under the urgency of events, they are prone to express their views by means of indirect confessions.

In the key scenes of *Stamboul Train,* a few of the same concerns which had already been introduced in Greene's first novels appear. Some new themes also appear, such as those of pity and modern politics. It's important to note, however, that the theme of sacrificial and redemptive love which was so prominent in *The Man Within* has been replaced by a pervasive disillusion. Most of the characters are seen to be morally hollow and emotionally dry. One or two may have a capacity for love or sacrifice. But they are pictured as the most helpless of victims. Thus Coral Musker, the younger dancer who is the one character exhibiting any real capacity for personal affection and loyalty, winds up in the suffocating clutches of the lesbian journalist. And Dr. Czinner, the idealistic revolutionary, dies of a gun shot wound in a shed. He had hoped to change the chaotic world where "the poor were starved and the rich were not happier for it . . . the thief might be punished or rewarded with titles . . . wheat was burned in Canada and coffee in Brazil, and the poor in his own country had no money for bread and froze to death in unheated rooms."[23]   But after his martyrdom, we see that his dream and sacrifice were totally futile.[24]

The death of Dr. Czinner is both the most riveting and the most worrisome thing about this novel. Many of the characters are treated like caricatures, and thus they can be ultimately dismissed as mere objects of satiric contempt. Dr. Czinner, on the other hand, is fleshed out sufficiently to take on real life. The result is that we begin to care for him as we can't for the other characters. Yet, at the end, he is shown to have led just as meaningless an existence as the rest. As a consequence, one might come away from this novel with the feeling that it's been a rousing story, but that there was nothing behind it except a profound disillusionment bordering on nihilism.

A Political Phase

The pervading sense of futility is even stronger in Greene's next book, *It's a Battlefield* (1934). With it, Greene entered a phase during which he wrote three troubling novels with specific political frameworks. The events of the first one are set off by the death of a policeman. This was an accident, since the Communist bus driver who killed him was just trying to defend his wife when a riot broke out at Hyde Park. Nevertheless, the driver is sentenced to death. The government, however, is nervous about carrying out the sentence because it is afraid of political repercussions. Thus it hesitates about what course to take, and while it does, the effect this situation has on the people directly or indirectly involved is brought out. Needless to say, justice isn't served in the end. Instead, the book leaves the impression that injustice is the unavoidable condition of the contemporary world.

This continues to be Greene's most unpopular book, and it's easy to see why. As if the subject of pervasive injustice weren't bleak enough, Greene adds such related themes as the perversion of love and the anguish of isolation. Moreover, as far as technique is concerned, he becomes so bold that he winds up with some confusing extravagancies. Having used a cinematic style with great success in *Stamboul Train,* he was bound to continue in this vein. Unfortunately, he now takes the idea of identifying the point-of-view with a ubiquitous camera eye so far that the story is sometimes too fragmented. Overlapping this problem is his experimentation with the stream-of-consciousness technique. There are occasions when he manages to use this method with great success, especially toward the end of the story when he attempts to link thought and action. At other times, though, he uses it so crudely that it's somewhat distracting.

It's indisputable, however, that in this novel Greene made important advances on several other fronts. He had taken the risk of populating a novel with many apparently unrelated people in his previous book, but there he used the simple device of the train to bring them together. This time he has taken just as many characters and set them adrift in London. But they are ultimately all joined together through several devices Greene had now mastered. The most significant of these are the employment of a circular, highly integrated plot structure; the use of vivid metaphors, similes, synecdoches, oxymorons, and other figures of speech to link the abstract with the concrete; the repetition of words which express the main themes; and the introduction of authorial comments.

As far as the latter point is concerned, it should be pointed out that Greene was something of a maverick.[25] While this novel was being written, modernism was a powerful new movement, and such former traditions as authorial comments in a novel were supposed to be on the way out. Greene, however, believed in the idea that behind a novel must stand the omniscient mind. When he set out to apply this idea, though, he wished to do it in a more subtle way than had usually been done in the past. The method he came up with was to bring out his views through the actions and thoughts of his characters, but in such an unobtrusive way that, barely revealing there has been a transitional shift, he makes us accept the words as those of one of his characters while at the same time making us feel the power of the greater expressiveness and wisdom which emanates from an authorial voice.[26] Because Greene uses this technique with very great skill, *It's a Battlefield* acquires a depth and thematic resonance it wouldn't otherwise have. At the same time it should be added that in this book the authorial voice expresses nothing but despair.[27]

The tone of despair in *England Made Me* (1935)[28] doesn't at first appear as strong as it was in *It's a Battlefield.* Yet this is only a temporary illusion due primarily to two factors. Greene now employs more deflecting irony than was his previous habit, and he places the political scene behind a story of love. This story, however, is hardly an ordinary love story. It involves a brother and sister and their confused feelings of incestuous love. As their story unfolds, we begin to see that in this novel Greene is exploring abnormal psychology because it's something which fascinates him. Yet at the same time we begin to understand that the incestuous, doomed love story is in a way a reflection of the times. It's the 1930's, and these are the years of incestuous corruption in international business, of depression in Europe, and, even though no direct mention is made of this in the novel, of the rise of Hitler.[29] Consequently, a person like the brother, who is characterized as being too innocent, has no real chance. He is doomed to die a victim of someone like the financial tycoon for whom his sister works and whose mistress she had become. He simply had no real chance in a world where, as his sister says at the end of the book, everybody steals while "giving nothing back" and where there is no such thing as "brotherhood in our boat. Only who can cut the biggest dash and who can swim."[30]

In several ways this is Greene's most successful novel up to this point. The counterpoints between love and betrayal, greed and politics are effectively drawn. The two main levels of the plot are clearly integrated. The setting is brilliantly wrought.[31] The movement and pacing of the story are charged with great energy.[32] And, unlike in the past, the multiple shifts between points-of-view almost invariably are brought off without any confusion.

Nevertheless, Greene was now fast approaching an impasse in his art. Since *Stamboul Train* he had steadily improved upon his stylistic techniques. But the same couldn't be said for his creation of protagonists. However vividly drawn, they tended to have the flatness of caricatures instead of the depth of fully realized characters. Evidently sensing this, Greene tried the extensive use of interior monologue in *England Made Me* to get inside his major characters. The results, at best, were only partially successful.[33] The combination of this self-conscious literary technique and Greene's instinctively sensual, direct, and subjective approach just wouldn't go together very well. There are times, in fact, when this combination takes away from the impact of the story because it seems as if Greene is straining too much to make this point with style. Fortunately, Greene learned from this unhappy experiment, and thus he more or less abandoned the use of interior monologue as a primary means of character development in his future novels. Instead, he would begin to write stories which tended to center on a protagonist who is developed by means of reflective minor characters, plot line, dialogue, figurative language, and such additional refined means as dreams.

Before Greene published his next novel, *A Gun for Sale* (1936),[34] he took the crucial trip to Africa during which he made the discovery that he actually had a love for life. As a result, his fiction began to take on a different quality. *A Gun for Sale* is in most ways still typical of what had gone before. As far as style is concerned, there are no real departures from past practices. The startling use of surrealism may be noted, but this is more a refinement than a change in Greene's technique. With respect to themes, several of those which had always concerned Greene are found in this book. He is still exploring such matters as betrayal, greed, injustice, violence, and political exploitation. However, when it comes to the central character and the effect he leaves on the story, there is an important difference. Unlike in the previous stories, the actions of the protagonist in *A Gun for Sale* ultimately give a certain meaning to his life and even hope to some of those who are affected by him.

At the beginning of this story, the protagonist, Raven, is pictured as a completely cold-blooded person who has no qualms at all about murdering an idealistic minister for pay. But once he is betrayed by his employers, and he sets out to revenge himself while at the same time running from the law, he starts to look more sympathetic. We begin to see him not only as a malevolent criminal but also as a victim, and finally as a kind of instrument of social justice. During the course of the double chase, we discover that there are things about his past which help to explain his violent behavior. Also, after he involves a girl in his desperate actions, we begin to see that he has a capacity to be emotionally influenced by other people. Finally, when he catches up to those who have betrayed him and kills them, before being shot himself, he becomes a kind of judicial scourge. For in killing them, he has saved society from people who were trying to force a war so that their armaments industry would thrive.

If one looks forward two years to the publication of *Brighton Rock,* it seems as if *A Gun for Sale* might have been a kind of preliminary study for it. There are a number of correspondences between the two books. The most striking of these is that Raven and Pinkie Brown, the protagonist of the later book, have so much in common as far as their past and present ways of life are concerned.[35] There is one big difference between them, though. Raven is running from his past and from the law. These forces are also after Pinkie. But the most powerful force which is in pursuit of him is that of religious salvation. Because of the injection of this extra dimension, *Brighton Rock* will turn out to be without a doubt a more distinguished book than anything Greene had written before.

Another Direction

It might be said that with the publication of *A Gun for Sale* Greene ended his formative period. He had now developed a highly distinctive style, and though he would continue to try to sharpen it, he wouldn't change it in any significant way. As for subject matter, he had by now introduced a number of themes which he would continue to investigate in an obsessive manner. Of these concerns, politics began to dominate. It's tempting, consequently, to speculate what would have happened if he had left it at that, if, that is, *A Gun for Sale* had turned out to be not the end but a continuing part of a phase. Would Greene today be remembered primarily as a writer of political thrillers set in the 1930's, a member of the Auden generation overshadowed by the poets of that time? It's not unlikely.

If Greene's reputation as a distinct and major writer is now assured, it's because after *A Gun for Sale* he would begin to write books which are directed toward salvation. Starting with *Brighton Rock,* he would write a series of so-called Catholic novels in which he explores the means of theological salvation. He tries a variety of angles, but they actually come down to a basic scheme. The focus is on protagonists who, at the beginning of their stories, are living in states of anxiety and decadence. Then, as their stories unfold, they begin to find their way to at least a glimpse of the redeeming light of God. More specifically, these novels end with the suggestion that grace has been the ultimate means of salvation, not primarily because the characters have been spiritually responsive, but because of the haunting mercy of God. The persistent and mysterious action of grace in the Catholic novels is what most clearly sets them apart from those that follow.

Beginning with the appearance of *The Quiet American* in 1955, Greene's major novels start to take on a secular slant. Like their religious counterparts, the protagonists in these later novels all appear to be doomed at first, and like them they manage to find their way to at least a glimmer of the possibility of salvation. But now this process leads to earthly and personal salvation. To get them to this end, Greene prefers to employ a basic pattern which, again, is similar to what is found in the Catholic novels. In his most recent novel he will try something a bit different, perhaps. Until then, his method in general is to start out by describing moribund men living in festering isolation and psychic dissolution, then follow them closely as they manage to escape, for however fleeting a moment, their private egoistical hells by learning to become imaginatively engaged with other human beings. The patterns of their regeneration are all complex, but on the whole it can be said that they take emotional and spiritual journeys which purge them and lead them toward a clearer self-understanding and a fuller and more compassionate vision of life.

III.
THE CATHOLIC NOVELS

When Greene set out to write *Brighton Rock* (1938), his intention was to come up with a plain detective novel, not the theological thriller it turned out to be.[1] Although he had been a practicing Catholic for several years, he had up to this point kept his religion and profession clearly separated. Then two events shook Greene out of this position—the assault against religion by the socialists in Mexico and the attack by Franco against Republican Spain. Now Greene had to admit that, given the nature of the present world, it was no longer possible, at least not for him, to place religion and contemporary existence in different compartments. This discovery impelled him, in turn, to involve himself in the examination of how faith can affect action.[2] From then on, Greene would always be concerned with this subject to some extent in his major works. But it's especially prominent in the Catholic tetralogy which began with *Brighton Rock.*

Because this concern took over fully only after Greene had already started *Brighton Rock,* the book is slightly disjointed at one point.[3] The first of the seven parts of the story seems to be written in the vein of the pure detective novel Greene had originally in mind. Then the story shifts toward the theological perspective, and keeps to it relentlessly until the end. This shift, it should be emphasized, is not so pronounced as to call attention to itself. Nevertheless, there is a likelihood that, at least on a subliminal level, it brought on some of the uneasiness which can be discerned in the first reviews which met the book. At least in most of these reviews, it's apparent that the commentators didn't quite know what to make of the religious subject once it entered the story, and as a result they by and large directed their attention toward the melodrama of undeniably a sensational story.

The story is set in motion when Pinkie Brown, a seventeen year old hoodlum, and his gang decide to kill Fred Hale because the latter's act of betrayal has led to the death of Kite, the previous leader of the mob. Trying to escape the killers, Hale attaches himself to Ida Arnold, a big-hearted sex figure who specializes in fun. But when she excuses herself momentarily to relieve herself of too much ale and to have a quick wash, the gang murders Hale. When Ida later reads in the newspapers about the mysterious circumstances surrounding Hale's death, she decides to investigate. As she begins closing in on Pinkie, he murders a nervous member of the gang and marries a young girl who knows too much about the true facts of Hale's violent death in order to avoid the possibility of her testifying against him in court. Driven into a panic by an accumulation of menacing circumstances, he decides that Rose must go, too. He thinks of a way to trick her into committing suicide; however, before he can succeed, Ida and her retinue arrive in time to save Rose. And Pinkie falls to a ghastly death over a cliff as he runs screaming from them.

All this, of course, is just the surface of the story. Underneath the melodrama, the dominant concern is profoundly religious. As the book starts to unfold, it becomes apparent that the major struggle is not between the forces of society and crime but between good and evil. This may be an age-old subject. What distinguishes this book from any number of other, more pious ones is that this struggle takes place primarily within a character who seems to take the risk of willingly damning himself despite his Catholic conscience. Not too long after the appearance of the novel, these issues began to replace the story's melodramatic qualities as the focus of critical attention. Nevertheless, even after all these years, Greene's first major novel remains his most widely misread.

This, ironically, is in large part the fault of Greene himself. Sometime after the publication of *Brighton Rock,* Greene made a careless remark to the effect that the novel was about a character who was bound for hell. He later tried to qualify this view by adding that what he "really meant was that . . . *Brighton Rock* is written in such a way that people could plausibly imagine that Pinkie went to hell, and then I cast doubt upon it in the ending."[4] Unfortunately, by then his earlier remark had, it appears, been accepted as the absolute truth by too many people.

The most influential of these was doubtless Evelyn Waugh. Evidently accepting Greene's earlier comment as simple fact, he came to the conclusion that *Brighton Rock* "challenged the soft

modern mood by creating a completely damnable youth. Pinkie
. . . is the ideal examinee for entry to Hell. He gets a pure alpha
on every paper."[5]   And this view has, more or less, persisted until
this day.

Looking at the structure of the action of *Brighton Rock,*
one would tend to agree that Pinkie seems clearly destined for
damnation. He appears to progress steadily in the maliciousness
and cruelty of his acts. Evidence can even be found that he per-
verts one by one the seven sacraments in the seven sections of
the book.[6] Hence there are critics who have concluded that he
is a sort of "juvenile Satan."[7]   And there are many critics who
agree with the one who finds that Pinkie progressively "descends
in stature throughout the work, until at the end he is damned for
all eternity."[8]

If there is an apparent structure of damnation, however,
there runs counter to it a subtle but impressive pattern of salvation. For one thing, Greene persuades us often enough that we
should take into consideration as an extenuating circumstance
the background of Pinkie. This is not to say that Greene is writing a sociological tract about the deterministic influence of the
past in creating juvenile delinquency, but that natural environ-
ment is one of the factors to be considered when trying to evalu-
ate the fate of a human being. Therefore, it is significant that
Pinkie has lived in squalor and degradation for all of his life. As
a child he lived in the slums with parents whose only apparent
moments of escape from an existence of grinding poverty consisted of the sexual ritual on Saturday nights, performed in the same
room where the boy had to sleep. Not surprisingly, Pinkie became desperate to escape the horror of his surroundings. As a result he was deeply grateful when Kite rescued him and made
him a member of the mob. When Kite, who becomes a father
figure to the boy, is murdered, Pinkie seeks consoling revenge
while at the same time trying to perpetuate the memory of the
man who had given him a new life by retaining his sad and violent habits. What he has also retained throughout his mobster
years is a memory, however faint at times, of his Catholic up-
bringing. Within him there always exists the fearful realization
that he is on the road to hell but that there remains an omnipresent possibility of theological salvation.

This intense religious conviction is something that sets him
apart from a host of characters with whom we are forced to com-
pare him. It is part of Greene's scheme to imply through the de-

vice of contrast that Pinkie has qualities which make him at least as worthy of our fair estimation as the persons surrounding him. A descriptive passage is particularly revealing of Greene's intent in this connection:

> A negro wearing a bright striped tie sat on a bench in the Pavilion garden and smoked a cigar. Some children played touch wood from seat to seat, and he called out to them hilariously, holding his cigar at arm's length with an air of pride and caution, his great teeth gleaming like an advertisement. They stopped playing and stared at him, backing slowly. He called out to them again in their own tongue, the words hollow and unformed and childish like theirs, and they eyed him uneasily and backed further away. . . . A band came up the pavement . . . , a blind band playing drums and trumpets, walking in the gutter, feeling the kerb with the edge of their shoes, in Indian file. You heard the music a long way off, persisting through the rumble of the crowd, the shots of exhaust pipes, and the grinding of the buses starting uphill for the racecourse.[9]

The absurd medley that is heard is the music of a spere where too many persons are, unlike Pinkie, blind to their direction. And the suspicious hilarity of the gaudy, alien man insinuates the truth about such people as Colleoni, the successful businessman-crook who was earlier depicted as one who "clinked very gently as he moved" in a plush ambience consisting of mechanical young men and their "small tinted creatures, who rang like expensive glass when they were touched but who conveyed an impression of being as sharp and tough as tin" (*BR,* p. 73). Later we see Sylvie, the moll of the recently dead Spicer, who "literally ran . . . towards the dark car-park and the game" less because she was excited by the reluctant advances of Pinkie than because of her love for a Lancia (*BR,* p. 166). Such people have very little to lose—perhaps a bit of money or time. Pinkie, on the other hand, is always intensely aware that he has a soul at stake.

It is especially this point that should be kept in mind when Pinkie is compaed to Ida, who at first appears to be a generous earth goddess wishing only to comfort and please her admirers. Her big, friendly breasts promise security and warmth; but they have actually destroyed many an adventurer with their false promises. She is a siren, alluring and powerful in the flesh but hollow in spirit. We are told that she "wasn't religious. She didn't believe in heaven or hell, only in ghosts, ouja boards, tables which rapped and little inept voices speaking plaintively of flowers" (*BR,* p. 40). Her philosophy and creed consisted of a remorseless mathematical formula: "An eye for an eye. . . . And vengeance and reward—they both were fun" (*BR,* p. 42). She stalks Pinkie not because she cares about what he did to Hale or what he might do to Rose. The hunt itself, not the people concerned, is what matters to her.

Ida's remorseless pursuit of Pinkie accentuates the progress of despair that her prey undergoes. As he travels along his violent road, Pinkie yearns for the end, but he can't stop because he is driven by pressures beyond his control. While he is driven from crime to crime, his hunger for peace increases in proportion to his growing panic. He starts out with the death of Hale because, as he sees it then, there exists an incumbent need for exact revenge. But the way of violence does not become easier with each act. He experiences, instead, an ever growing panic that things are getting out of hand, emphasized by his repeated references to the refrain from the *Agnus Dei* calling for peace. Finally forced into the position at the end where he has evidently no way out but through more slaughter, he screams with horror: "My God, have I got to have a massacre?" (*BR,* p. 303).

The high emotion of these climactic words indicates how far Pinkie has come in the way of human feeling. In the early pages of the book he is pictured as thoroughly, even supernaturally, evil. He is described in serpentine terms, with a flickering tongue and venom coursing through his veins. His eyes are ancient and icy, as of those in whom "human feeling has died" (*BR,* p. 5). His face has a "starved intensity, a kind of hideous and unnatural pride" (*BR,* p. 4). This infernal pride is the source of his murderous strength, for it allows him to be totally unconcerned about anyone else. Other people mean nothing to him because his "imagination hadn't awoken. . . . He couldn't see through other people's eyes, or feel with their nerves" (*BR,* p. 52). However, in the central section of the novel there is a reversal scene of sorts, for here Pinkie, facing the imminent possibility of his own death, goes through a process of humiliation and humility during which we see him weep, try to pray, and even think momentarily of confession and giving a holy statue to the church by way of atonement for his past.

It is of course true that Pinkie does not in reality fully repent just yet, nor does he feel lasting remorse, since he rationalizes that there was no time for such resolutions while he was on the run. Nevertheless, the experiences of this crisis will leave a lasting effect on him. After these moments when he is forced to fully face his own character and fate, he will be capable of being shocked by his own cruelty in pushing the blind band out of his way on one occasion. Also, after this crisis Pinkie has moments when he has a strong sense of nostalgia for an imagined innocence of the past and a yearning for his own annihilation. And it's remarkable how he begins to feel a need to understand other people. When he goes to see his lawyer at his wretched home, he is shaken by a new experience. Pinkie "had never known Prewitt like this before: it was a frightening and an entrancing exhibition. A man was coming alive before his eyes: he could see the nerves set to work in the agonised flesh, thought bloom in the transparent brain" (*BR*, p. 262). He had come to see Prewitt because of his immense self-concern; but when he leaves, he is thinking of the lawyer's life of putrefaction. Even more significant, though is the development of some affection for Rose.

What really matters in Greene's world is whether or not his characters experience a change of heart; and this happens to Pinkie, however slow and reluctant the process, most clearly in his relations with Rose. At first he only looks on her with intense hatred as another obstacle to safety from the law. After the reversal scene, however, he begins to experience certain feelings for Rose that are new and surprising to him. It's clear that he will grow ever more desperate to destroy her, since she represents not only a dangerous witness but also the marriage trap. Yet concurrently she sparks a hint of imaginative sympathy in him. He is touched by her loyalty to him when he goes to her for aid after being cut up and nearly bleeding to death at the race track. The pure hatred that he had felt for Rose when she reminded him of Nelson Place becomes a faint feeling of longing for her and what she represented when he sees her face up to Ida in his behalf and an obscure sense of humility when she thereafter swears her eternal fidelity to him. When he goes to her parents to bargain for their daughter's hand, he feels a touch of pity for Rose because of her inability to escape the trap of poverty. After the sad marriage, he is ready to defend her against Cubitt's innocent yet painful marriage humor to such an extent that he startles himself: "An extraordinary indignation jerked in the

Boy's brain and fingers. It was almost as if someone he loved had been insulted" (*BR*, p. 184). During their wretched honeymoon he can experience the beginnings of tenderness, and instead of the anticipated revulsion he reacts with faint sensation of fondness when they consummate their marriage.

It is true that all too soon Pinkie begins to plan to get rid of Rose once and for all; but this is possibly because he now fears that these growing feelings of affection will drain him of his venomous strength. He is clearly perplexed and frightened by the discovery that he was becoming involved in someone else's character and fate. Understandably, when the time comes to go through with the plan for the death of Rose, his feelings undergo an intensity which illustrates the agonizing paradox of the situation. He must be rid of her; yet he knows that she had somehow broken his habit of hate: "It was quite true—he hadn't hated her; he hadn't even hated the act. There had been a kind of pleasure, a kind of a pride, a kind of—something else" (*BR*, p. 299). This is the closest indication that Pinkie has at least a rudimentary experience of love.

One does not, however, have to prove that Pinkie actually goes beyond these stirrings of love for Rose in the metaphysical framework of this book. It is obvious that Rose loves Pinkie—in fact to such an extent that she flirts with suicide, the worst imaginable sin to her since she is also a Catholic, to show her readiness to do anything for him. Since Rose, like Greene's later heroine in *The End of the Affair,* is a repository of sacred love, she becomes a powerful factor in the process of salvation. Having followed the example of Christ's redemptive suffering, she contains within her mysterious powers of forgiveness. She is the clearest and most compelling representative of what Greene imagines as the omnipresent and appalling force of grace.

Significantly enough, the story begins on Whitsun, which celebrates the descent of the Holy Spirit. Then we are reminded of the presence of grace through several reappearing images and symbols. The recurring rhythmic pressure of the wind, tide, and rain act as unobtrusive symbols of the nature of grace. The frequent wail of music functions as a painful reminder to Pinkie of his primary season of peace, specifically when he was a choirboy. Subtly imposed is a montage sequence of an old man and a seagull which suggests God's complex and protean mercy. In a key passage grace is, by implication, pictured as immensely patient and gentle and capable of disturbing consequences:

> An old man went stooping down the shore, very slowly, turning the stones, picking among the dry seaweed for cigarette ends, scraps of food. The gulls which stood like candles down the beach rose and cried under the promenade. The old man found a boot and stowed it in his sack and a gull dropped from the parade and swept through the iron nave of the Palace Pier, white and purposeful in the obscurity: half-vulture and half-dove (*BR*, p. 161).

Grace, like the old man, patiently picks among the rubble of humanity for anything that might be redeemed. And, like the gull, it is purposeful in a mysterious way, both a bird of prey and of peace. This paradoxical nature of grace is what we see when it is pictured at the moment of its greatest pressure, when it tempts Pinkie as he drives toward the planned death of Rose:

> An enormous emotion beat on him; it was like something trying to get in; the pressure of gigantic wings against the glass. Dona nobis pacem. He withstood it, with all the bitter force of the school bench, the cement playground, the St. Pancras waiting-room, Dallow's and Judy's secret lust, and the cold unhappy moment on the pier. If the glass broke, if the beast—whatever it was—got in, God knows what it would do. He had a sense of huge havoc— the confession, the penance and the sacrament—and awful distraction, and he drove blind into the rain (*BR*, p. 300).

Pinkie withstands its force here. Yet whether this means that God's grace ever gives up on him is a different question because, as the priest at the end tells Rose in words which can serve as the coda of this and Greene's other Catholic novels, "You can't conceive, my child, nor can I or anyone the . . . appalling . . . strangeness of the mercy of God" (*BR*, p. 308).

Consequently, when we see Pinkie during his last moments on earth, it is not at all certain that he is about to enter hell. Rather than being pictured as an infernal figure, he finally appears like a child, "badgered, confused, betrayed"; and he is not expanded with Satanic pride but shrinks "into a schoolboy flying in panic and pain, scrambling over a fence, running on" (*BR*, p. 304). His agony is hellish as the vitriol steams on his face and, fetus like, he folds in terrible pain. In the context of the total picture of his life, however, it's clear that these are the last in a long series of agonies on earth, a life which has certainly been an utter hell for him, thus actually cancelling out the need for another one. Therefore, when Pinkie seems to be "withdrawn suddenly by a hand out of any existence—past or present," he is significantly "whipped away into zero—nothing" (*BR*, p. 304), perhaps that restful vacancy which he had yearned for so intensely, if God has as much mercy as Greene imagines and as a writer he was always inclined to reveal.

Brighton Rock is the clearest example of what was becoming one of Greene's habitual schemes. This was to begin a book by focusing on a protagonist who initially strikes us as very unsympathetic, and then to force our attitudes to undergo a fundamental change. Because of Greene's penchant for the harsh delineation of the flaws in his characters, this process of adjustment can be exceedingly reluctant on our part. Yet it's obvious that Greene actually wants us to undergo a real struggle. Without it, he seems to imply, our sympathetic understanding is bound to be shallow, incomplete, or merely sentimental. Moreover, without such a process of engagement, the stories wouldn't be effective on a level which is most important to Greene—to reveal something essential of the reader to himself. The challenge to do this happens to be most extreme in the case of Pinkie Brown. But it is apparent throughout Greene's major work, and it certainly has considerable intensity in his next Catholic novel, *The Power and the Glory*.

Before Greene brought out *The Power and the Glory* in 1940, he published two more books. One, *The Confidential Agent* (1939), was in fact written at the same that *The Power and the Glory* was taking shape. It's obvious where Greene's main effort went. *The Power and the Glory* turned out to be the most accomplished of the Catholic tetralogy, and to many people Greene's masterpiece. *The Confidential Agent,* on the other hand, was in several ways Greene's least satisfactory book since his first ones.

The trouble is not with the story, for it's undeniably gripping. Using a thriller pattern, Greene focuses on an agent from a foreign government who has come to England to negotiate a coal contract. His mission is desperately urgent because the coal is needed to continue a civil war struggle back home. As soon as he lands in England, however, serious problems begin to beset him. The most ironic is that his government doesn't really have confidence in him. But, even aside from that, treachery follows him like a disease wherever he goes. That is, with one important exception. There is a girl who manages to inspire a measure of trust and love in him through her example. As a consequence, although he fails to fulfill his political mission, he begins to re-gain his capacity for human emotions at the end.

If Greene's primary attention hadn't been elsewhere, *The Confidential Agent* might have turned out to be one of his better efforts. Nowhere else is he smoother or more consistent in applying certain techniques. The employment of a circular structure, a deliberate point-of-view, and an impressionistic atmosphere are thoroughly commendable. Also, the presenta-tion of such themes as the importance of trust and the contagion of war is effectively direct. On the other hand, Greene hardly bothers to get below the surface of his characters. And this, in turn, is due to what appears to be the major problem with the book. It's written in a curiously detached way.[10] At one point in the story, Greene has his protagonist think that he "was damned like a creative writer to sympathy" for "other people's pain, their lives, their individual despairs."[11] In his most suc-cessful novels, Greene undergoes just this kind of wrenching pas-sion, but it's missing in *The Confidential Agent.*

The other book which was published in 1939, *The Lawless Roads,*[12] was Greene's second travel book. Unlike *Journey Without a Map,* this travel book gives us little insight into the paradoxical mind of the writer. It was a commissioned book on the religious persecution going on in Mexico in the spring of 1938, and this is what Greene set out to describe with a report-er's eye. While he was observing the political and physical condi-tions around him, however, the novelist in him was sometimes at least subconsciously at work. As a result, he sprinkled his ac-count with the depiction of a number of interesting characters he met during his trip. Several of these characters, in turn, found their way into the pages of *The Power and the Glory.* And one who didn't actually provide Greene with the subject for his next novel by recounting a story a "whiskey" priest who had been so drunk during a baptism that he insisted on christening a boy Brigitta.[13]

The Power and the Glory

In a sense, *The Power and the Glory* (1940) is a kind of sequel to *Brighton Rock,* since it also may fall under the heading of an eschatological thriller. However, there is at the same time a fundamental difference which should be pointed out at the start. If there is any doubt that Pinkie goes to hell, there is none that the priest in *The Power and the Glory* is destined for heaven. At the conclusion of this novel we are left with the peculiar feeling that we have been following the progress of a saint. We do, in fact, have in this book a strikingly contemporary hagiography. The priest's painful way to sainthood has been marked with fear, betrayal, and temptations especially typical of modern society. When we first see him, he is trying to escape the terrors of a political state. But gradually we come to see clearly with and through him that, as far as Greene was concerned, our mundane existence is naturally infernal, and that the only way to truly find peace is by means of a guiding vision of heaven.

The man-made political hell which appears to be abandoned by God is Mexico of the 1930's, where the government had decided to stamp out Catholicism and to erect in its place socialism and atheism as guiding principles. God's power appears to be impotent against the new politics that demand of the priests who have not already fled either betrayal of the church or execution. When the story opens, it seems that the government has indeed been highly successful in its campaign since the church buildings stand empty of worshippers and the priesthood has all but disappeared. Only one priest seems to be left, and he looks to be merely a grotesque parody of his vocation because he has a terrible weakness for the various sins of the flesh and he appears to be inept at performing his duties. Yet because he has remained, the atheistic state, vividly emobied by a lieutenant, feels compelled to hunt him down. The priest manages to continue to evade the lieutenant and his men for some time, even though they come face to face twice. And after his prolonged flight the priest even succeeds in crossing the border to a more tolerant state where he can find sanctuary. He is lured back across the border, however, in order to give confession to a dying gangster, even though he knows full well that a trap laid by the state is surely waiting for him. After he is indeed captured, little time expires before the morning of his execution. As he faces his death and looks back on his life, he feels that he has been a terrible disappointment to

God. And when he does not succeed in being given confession by another frightened priest, it appears to him that damnation is his due. From a doctrinal point of view, the priest dies in a state of eternal damnation. However, as the structure and texture of the story show, salvation does not depend on formulas or even deeds, but on faith and ultimately on God's mercy.

To emphasize the thrust of his story, Greene took some calculated risks. This time he was writing a novel initially controlled both by a preconceived theme and genre. In order to work within these narrow bounds, he had to devise a strategy which would turn the constriction to his advantage. What he came up with was almost the perfect solution. While using the thriller pattern as a basic structural pattern, he cast the moral burden of the priest into a parable and populated the story with stark, flat characters who would take on life mainly by the way they contrasted with each other and, additionally, by the way the brilliantly depicted setting reflected upon them. This scheme is so fully under the control of Greene that sometimes the novel suffers from a kind of rigidity. Nevertheless, there is no denying that what the story loses in spontaneity it more than makes up in intensity, and that this intensity is of a rare kind. No one, not even Dostoevsky, could have written a more hypnotic, feverish book about guilt, love, and redemption.

Not surprisingly, there are various ways in which one might trace the priest's arduous journey from corruption to redemption, for in Greene's Catholic novels the *way* to God is what is aesthetically interesting to him. The surface story, of course, suggests an intricate thriller in which the hunt motif operates in revealing the thematic design. Our first view of the priest tells us that he is a fugitive trying to escape from the pursuing forces of the political state; but then we discover with him that he is even more intensely pursued by the power of grace. When the priest encounters most directly the persistent nature of grace, that is, when he finds out that he is compelled to re-cross the border even though it will surely mean his capture, he surrenders to God once and for all and accepts his destiny. At the same time, now no longer the quarry of either the state or God, he becomes the spiritual hunter of the lieutenant who begins to feel haunted after he has several discussions with the priest. Thus there is a criss-cross pattern to be discovered in a book filled with cross motifs and images. Naturally the Christian cross dominates this story of a priest whose way parallels and meets at many points the path of Christ to his crucifixion.[14] From another angle one can discover Danteian circles.[15] Or one can find the parabolic curve of a Greek tragedy.[16] In fact, there seem to be as many patterns to be found as there are angles of observation. Still, if such patterns exist in the story, the basic way to measure the tortuous progress of the priest is to recognize that he carries his spiritual fidelity like a temptation among various contrasting characters.

In other words, during his pilgrimage the priest meets a succession of people who serve to signify to him and to us the various sides of his nature and whose chronological accumulation suggests the distance he already has and has yet to travel. Accordingly, the first person that we see him with is one who feels abandoned and has hopes of escape. His name, Tench, comes near to spelling out the aroma of his occupation and his condition. He is a dentist who dreams of leaving this festering land, whose physical and spiritual condition is made concrete by the ever-present scavengers and by the rotting teeth, which are the source of Tench's income and his view of human corruption. While he literally spends his life gazing into the depths of human decay, he dreams of escape. But, unlike the priest, he is more concerned with saving his pesos than his soul. Following the brief encounter during which each has dwelled on his entrapment, Tench gazes after the boat which pulls away from his wretched town with romanticized feelings of huge despair. But the priest, who had hoped to get on the boat only to be drawn back into the interior by a personal and, one suspects, heavenly summons, realizes in his disappointment as he prays to be caught that there can be no escape for him since he is still a servant of his people and of God.

Coral, a young girl of 13 years who is a willing slave of her hypochondriac mother and childish father, represents the priest's next significant encounter. Although, as she informs the priest, she is an atheist who lost her religious faith at age 10, she possesses an immense sense of responsibility for those who seem to need her. Similar to the developing feelings of the priest, she was "ready to accept any responsibility . . . without a second thought. It was her life."[17] When the priest is later forced to go back to the village where, in a moment of despair, he had lain with a woman, he is once more confronted by his experience of lust in the person of Maria and by the issue of his momentary despair in the form of Brigida, his child. When he sees his daughter for the first time in six years, he feels as if he were "seeing his own mortal sin look back at him, without contrition" (*PAG,* p. 77). He agonizes over the conviction that she was fated for corruption upon discovering that the "world was in her heart already, like the small spot of decay in a fruit" (*PAG,* p. 95). And so, shaken by a certainty that she was without protection, he offers a fearfully unselfish prayer: "O God, give my any kind of death—without contrition, in a state of sin—only save this child" (*PAG,* p. 95). It is while he thinks of her in these sacrificial terms that he approaches the discovery of the nature of God's love—that is, that "one must love every soul as if it were one's own child" (*PAG,* p. 96). Being human, he feels his love "tethered and aching" for Brigida (*PAG,* p. 96); yet he is ultimately powerless to offer her sanctuary. Nevertheless, he has come to the point where he can imagine the radiance of divine love.

The maturation of his Christian understanding of divine love is illustrated during his next significant encounter, which is with a mestizo who, he soon realizes, will be his Judas. Instead of reacting with hatred and self-pity, he looks at himself closely and sees that he, too, has had the capacity for evil—not only to betray but also to feed on ambition, pride, lust, greed, and love of authority. No one should be beyond charitable thoughts, he thinks, for "Christ had died for this man too" (*PAG,* p. 117). When the priest looks at a man now, he can think of what is central to his faith, the "convincing mystery—that we were made in God's image. God was the parent, but He was also the policeman, the criminal, the priest, the maniac, and the judge. Something resembling God dangled from the gibbet or went into odd attitudes before the bullets in a prison yard or contorted itself like a camel in the attitude of sex" (*PAG,* p. 119). At this point his extraordinary vision of love is complete, and he can feel charity for any sinner he meets thereafter.

Because he has been going through a process of purgation, he is ready for an apocalypse which serves to dramatize his spiritual progress. That experience takes place during a night in a jail cell, where he finds himself among prisoners who function to represent both his past sins and mankind in general. When he is made to enter, he asks, "Who are these people?" However, before he leaves he knows that they are intimately related to him through the ties of sin and that they are to be pitied, not hated, since hate "was just a failure of imagination" (*PAG,*

p. 157). That they are in jail only serves to symbolize the nature of this life to him, for this place was really "very like the world: overcrowded with lust and crime and unhappy love, it stank to heaven; but . . . after all it was possible to find peace there, when you knew for certain that the time was short" (*PAG*, p. 149). Ironically, because he is passed off by the police as a mere derelict who has been caught with some illegal spirits, he will be dismissed the next morning. But though he escapes this time, he will thereafter be drawn back to the memory of this night when he experienced an extraordinary feeling of fellowship for and identification with a communion of sinners. The place is filled with carnality, wrath, false pride, and various other sins; but he can now discover beauty even here, as he tells the pious woman complaining about the sounds of lust in a corner:

> Such a lot of beauty. Saints talk about the beauty of suf-
> fering. Well, we are not saints, you and I. Suffering to us
> is just ugly. Stench and crowding and pain. *That* is beau-
> tiful in that corner—to them. It needs a lot of learning to
> see things with a saint's eye: a saint gets a subtle taste for
> beauty and can look down on poor ignorant palates like
> theirs. But we can't afford to (*PAG*, pp. 155-156).

His overwhelming humility makes him giggle when it is suggested that he was a martyr, but we can see that he has the feelings of a saint although he cannot realize it.

After this night his immense humility, not his self-concern, is what actually forces him to continue to try to escape the civil authorities by fleeing to another state.[18] He believes that he is not good enough to stay because he sees himself as a continuing insult to God if he remains as a representative of the church. In time he finally does manage to cross the border and finds a place of refuge with the Lehrs. This is what he dreamed of at the beginning of the novel. Yet although the Lehrs live in a material paradise, he finds that their life cannot satisfy him. Lehr, too, is an exile who has successfully escaped civil oppression, and he now seems content with his major concern—being "cunning in the defence of the good life" (*PAG*, p. 192). However, as his German name suggests, his life, which is based on hedonistic satisfaction, is not edenic but quite empty. He and his sister lead lives of dignified order, but the ritual of their existence, like the index of the Gideon bible in their home, follows an absurd formula. Thus the priest finds himself suddenly possessed by a strange sense of nostalgia for the night in the cell. When the Judas figure materializes abruptly to lure him back across the border, his reaction is less shock than a kind of dumb relief. He had, after all, previously felt the temptation of self-sacrifice in a number of ways. One also recalls that he has been particularly drawn by the summons of children, who, it becomes apparent in the course of the book, come to symbolize both his lost innocence and the agency of grace. And although he could not then clearly define it as such, he had felt the growing force of grace through a series of epiphanies as he had approached the border from the other direction. Now the reappearance of the Judas figure to tempt him back was a clear indication that God, more than the lieutenant, was the hunter. Thus, even if he knows that capture awaits him, he "felt quite cheerful; he had never really believed in this peace. He had dreamed of it so often on the other side that now it meant no more to him than a dream [and] it was time he woke up" (*PAG,* p. 216). He goes back with the conviction that God's territory is the only sanctuary.

The lieutenant who waits for him in ambush is a secular counterpart of the priest. He is a mystic too, but "what he had experienced was vacancy—a complete certainty in the existence of a dying, cooling world, of human beings who had evolved from animals for no purpose at all" (*PAG,* p. 23). He can admire the quality of loyalty in the priest, but he can see no real meaning behind it. And as he tells the priest on the way back to the city and the execution, it seems that the priest's God is not even grateful for good service; to him it appears that in the case of the priest God has cruelly rewarded loyalty with punishment. But the priest's answer summarizes his willing acceptance of his fate and his awe of the mystery of God's grace:

> I don't know a thing about the mercy of God: I don't
> know how awful the human heart looks to Him. But I
> do know this—that if there's ever been a single man in
> this state damned, then I'll be damned too. . . . I wouldn't
> want it to be any different. I just want justice, that's all
> (*PAG,* p. 240).

The lieutenant, like the priest, dedicates his life to justice; but because his idealistic hope depends ultimately on imperfect men, it is, the novel tells us, doomed.

As the priest confronts his fate on the morning of his execution, he has doubts about whether he is even hell-worthy. We can see, however, that he is now clearly favored by God's grace. It is true that he has traveled a bizarre, convoluted road to sainthood—through the wilderness of human failure and the entanglements of his own heart. Yet there is no doubt that his final thoughts about his failures are deeply ironic for we can see that the priest has attained what he had no hope for: "He knew now that at the end there was only one thing that counted—to be a saint" (*PAG*, p. 253).

When Greene published his next book, *The Ministry of Fear* (1943), it might have seemed for a time that what can now be called his Catholic phase had ended. After all, this novel was conspicuously secular in nature,[19] and it was the only book Greene published for some eight years with the exception of a collection of short stories which were characterized more by psychological than religious concerns.[20] But when *The Heart of the Matter* finally appeared in 1948, it became evident in retrospect that *The Ministry of Fear* had been a kind of warm-up for the following novel.

In *The Ministry of Fear* Greene illustrates that with the onset of World War II there was no longer any doubt that "thrillers are like life."[21] The protagonist, Arthur Rowe, learns this fact while on the run from various dangers. Another of Greene's hunted men, he is most obviously threatened by the blitz of London and by some spies who have infested his country. More indirectly, and more significantly, he is also threatened by the assaults of contending emotions. The mainspring of his emotional terror goes back to an act of euthanasia. He had poisoned his dying wife, thinking to spare her from more pain. Since then, however, he has been haunted by severe remorse and doubts about his act. These feelings have grown to such an extent that at the beginning of the story his life seems paralyzed with guilt. Then, accidentally, he is thrust into a melodrama of political and moral confrontation, and this starts him on his way toward a kind of rebirth. By the end of what is orchestrated like a mixture of spy thriller and Jacobean revenge play, Rowe is still a somewhat haunted man. Yet he is emotionally alive again, having reached the point where he can love again, and, conversely, having learned what the paradoxical reflection between love and pity is. He has learned that pity is allied with cruelty and destruction, and that it may indeed be the "worst passion of all" (*MOF*, p. 206). At the same time, he has become convinced that the ministry of fear was "as large as life to which all who loved belonged. If one loved one feared" (*MOF*, p. 267).

This lesson represents the crux of *The Ministry of Fear.* Still, one can object that the novel suffers because the issues of pity and love don't arise naturally enough out of the drama. At times the impression is quite distinct that these thoughts are superimposed on the story, and this has the ultimate effect of undermining Rowe's believability as an exponent of the dangers of confusing love with pity. Fortunately, Rowe's story didn't represent Greene's last word on this subject. In his next novel, he created a protagonist who is again torn by these emotional factors. But this character's agony is depicted with much greater success.

The Heart of the Matter

If Rowe and Scobie, the protagonist of *The Heart of the Matter* (1948), have certain emotional preoccupations in common, they are at the same time very different. The essential difference, not surprisingly, is the fact that Scobie is a serious Catholic whose religion affects all of his emotions in a decisive way. Therefore, soon after the story gets under way, it becomes apparent that Rowe serves as his predecessor only in a thematic way. As far as his disposition is concerned, Scobie has much more in common with the whiskey priest. This does not mean that he is also headed for sainthood. Yet he does turn out to be a martyr of sorts, and a person of inviolable motives, despite the fact that he appears willingly to head toward his own damnation by committing suicide. At least as Scobie prepares for his death he is convinced that he is ensuring his doom. And clearly according to Catholic doctrine he dies in a state of mortal sin. Scobie's act is, however, not one of theological defiance but of deeply felt human self-sacrifice and compassion. Consequently, there remains the clear possibility of salvation, because, as the novel argues, God's love is profoundly receptive, especially when love is invoked.

Scobie's motives behind his act of hopelessness are what ultimately count. He does not commit the unforgiveable sin, as church doctrine calls it and he believes it to be, because his despair is less religious than psychological. He advances to his fate with the inevitability of a protagonist in a Greek tragedy.[22] As he finds himself being whirled in an ever-growing circle of despair,[23] to him there seems finally no way out except through self-destruction. To remain, he has decided, would mean that he would have to live with overwhelming feelings of guilt, cause immense unhappiness to the two women in his life, and bring outrageous pain to God.

What has driven Scobie to his unbearable impasse is a sinister quality that can devour one from within—pity. His heart goes out to all suffering humanity, but because pity feeds on pride rather than on humility, he is in danger of turning malignant with this dangerous emotion. Having the illusion of a virtue, pity is in reality what Auden describes as "that corrupt parody of love and compassion which is so insidious and deadly for sensitive natures."[24] In a novel the form of which is based on the eternal subject of triangular love, that emotion in its pure state is remarkably elusive. Although Scobie is hopelessly tied to his wife Louise and to his young mistress Helen, it is pity which is the link that matters for him, and it is pity that leads to his ultimate betrayal of them. And on the allegorical plane of the novel, where another triangle exists, Scobie is drawn to both Yusef, who comes to personify the infernal temptations, and to God by this same corrupt form of love. As in a morality play, the real drama will take place within the soul of the protagonist, with an evil genius pulling in one direction and God in the other. Divine love, however, proves powerful enough to embrace a debased kind of affection and to transform it into a higher form.

After fifteen years of marriage to Louise, it is a wretched victim of time Scobie sees when he looks at her, not a partner in life. She has been ravaged by the sudden death of an only child, by the hard life of a policeman's wife in an African colony, by the subtle decay of marriage, and by the thousand little defeats of her years. Life has been continuously disappointing to her, and this has weakened her endurance and has made her capable of monstrous cruelty and selfishness. Besides, time has devoured what beauty she once had, leaving her with an unnatural ugliness. But it is precisely when she is an image of helplessness and ugliness—"clutching one of his fingers like a child"[25] or appearing like "a joint under a meat cover" (*HOM*, p. 17)—that is, when Scobie sees her most clearly as a victim of a life which he imagines he has been essentially responsible for, that he comes closest to loving her:

> He watched her through the muslin net. Her face had the yellow-ivory tinge of atabrine: her hair, which had once been the colour of bottled honey, was dark and stringy with sweat. These were the times of ugliness when he loved her, when pity and responsibility reached the intensity of a passion. It was pity that told him to go: he wouldn't have woken his worst enemy from sleep—leave alone Louise (*HOM*, p. 16).

Scobie values sleep because it represents the time of peace, a form of escape from the terror of life, the little death. He thinks constantly of peace, yearning for it like a mystic for a vision. Ironically, even in sleep he is tormented by its promise. Once he dreamed that

> it had appeared to him as the great glowing shoulder of the moon heaving across his window like an iceberg, arctic and destructive in the moment before the world was struck; by day he tried to win a few moments of its company, crouched under the rusting handcuffs in the locked office, reading the reports from the sub-stations. Peace seemed to him the most beautiful word in the language; My peace I give you, my peace I leave with you: O Lamb of God, who takest away the sins of the world, grant us thy peace. In the Mass he pressed his fingers against his eyes to keep the tears of longing in (*HOM*, p. 61).

So when Louise begs him to find a way to send her to South Africa for a long rest, and later suggests that he will find peace once she is gone, he is tempted into making a rash promise of consent even though he has no idea how to get enough money together for such a trip.

This decision is his first step toward his fateful end. But even if Scobie could have known the consequences of this promise, he would have acted in the same way, for he was always ready to lift the burden of responsibility, especially when he came upon the suffering of children or child-like adults. Having been absent during the death of his own child, he has ever since felt irrationally guilty and has tried to atone for what he sees as his profound failure. Thus when he is confronted by the pleading of a Portuguese ship captain not to report his sentimental letter to his daughter that he has tried to get past the wartime censors, Scobie cannot resist giving in to such "an unattractive child, the fat boy of the school" (*HOM*, p. 49). The name of the ship is the *Esperanca;* ironically, it turns out to be the scene of an act that will lead to hopelessness. Here Scobie betrays the integrity of his profession for the first time, not for money but for sentiment, a very treacherous sort of corruption "because you couldn't name its price" (*HOM*, p. 55).

Scobie continues on the road to corruption when, because he can find no other quick means, he goes to Yusef, a shady Syrian merchant, to borrow the money for Louise's trip. Professional discretion demands that he not be under any kind of obligation to a man of Yusef's dubious reputation; however, he is prepared to go this far because he now feels the full weight of his wife's unhappiness. Besides, he is instinctively drawn to Yusef because here seems to be someone else to be pitied. He is one of the unattractive, lonely rejects of life who, it has been Scobie's experience, are fated to be abused. Scobie is deceived, though, when he imagines Yusef to be just another innocent victim of life. Instead, it's Yusef who victimizes others by feeding on and living for business profit, as symbolized by his gold teeth that "flashed instantaneously like a torch" (*HOM*, p. 29). The setting of the loan transaction with Scobie tells us more about Yusef's true nature: "The bungalow was divided into a succession of small rooms identically furnished with sofas and cushions and low tables for drinks like the rooms in a brothel" (*HOM*, p. 158). Its decoration is even more significant, for it reveals that Greene's purpose is to imply that Yusef is a satanic character. The "hideous mauve silk cushions, the threads showing where the damp was rotting the covers: the tangerine curtains . . . the blue siphon of soda" add up to a suggestion of "an eternal air like the furnishings of hell" (*HOM*, p. 159). What seduced Scobie into this unnatural union was the promise of peace. But although he gets the money, the price he pays in return amounts to very nearly the loss of his soul, or at least its temporary defilement.

One should note, by the way, that the affair between Scobie and Yusef is described in highly sexual terms. This is not intended to imply that Yusef's attraction to Scobie is mainly physical but is rather meant to symbolize the corrupt form of Yusef's emotion. His "love" for Scobie is the opposite extreme of pity—adoration. As the story tells us, this kind of blind worship of a man is just as sinister and dangerous as pity. Evidently because Yusef's antithetical kind of affection promises rest from responsibility, Scobie cannot resist it. And because he is seduced by its force, he will thereafter be tormented by feelings of self-disgust and self-betrayal. Yusef, who comes to represent evil genius, will continue to try to entice him until the time arrives when the power of God's spirit proves to be more potent and Scobie decides he must destroy his own corruption.

After finally seeing Louise off, Scobie looks forward to coming back to an empty house. However, Yusef materializes that night to offer him his debased friendship and to trick him into framing a competing Syrian merchant. Not long thereafter Helen will come into his life. Again he will be drawn to her because of the sentiment of pity. As she is brought ashore on a stretcher, having endured dreadful suffering after her ship was torpedoed by a submarine, his heart goes out to her for he cannot resist such a picture of human wreckage:

> The face was ugly with exhaustion: the skin looked as though it were about to crack over the cheekbones: only the absence of lines showed that it was a young face. . . . Her arms as thin as a child's lay outside the blanket, and her fingers clasped a book firmly, Scobie could see the wedding-ring loose on her dried-up finger (*HOM*, p. 125).

We realize, of course, that the loose ring is an indication adultery was being carried into Scobie's life. He will later be eager to merely befriend her, since they seem to have important qualities in common—she informs him that she, too, is a loner, hates complexity and complicity, and can talk about death without reservation. But it is the image of her child-like weakness and ugliness that lures and then traps Scobie into a fateful kiss that shatters his illusion of safety from involvement. The fact is that he has only shed one responsibility to assume another. Helen is naturally much younger than Louise; but since she is not essentially different from her in other respects, this new relationship will take the same road to unhappiness, with Scobie increasingly controlled by the feeling that it is his responsibility to save Helen from the various disappointments of life.

Consequently, when Louise unexpectedly decides to return upon learning that there are rumors flying about her husband and a young woman, Scobie finds it impossible to suddenly desert his mistress.   And since he cannot give up his wife either, he is caught in an intolerable dilemma.   He tries to maintain his dual role of husband and lover, but the results are predictably disastrous.   He has a terrible scene with Helen in which she accuses him of hypocrisy when he tells her that he could never marry her because his religion forbids divorce.   In her hysteria she screams at him to go to hell, and indeed his path seems to him to lead there.   Ironically, a priest comes to see him soon thereafter because of a feeling Scobie can be of comfort at a time when the fear of impotency in saving souls is overwhelming.   Then a series of other events accumulate during one day to suggest a quickly closing trap.   Wilson, who has been spying on Scobie's activities partly because it is his war-time job to check on security but mainly because he imagines that he loves Louise, leaves a cryptic note in Scobie's office which, characteristic of his ineptitude, fails to hide the fact that he has gone so far as to start checking his rival's files.   Scobie finds out that, in a cruel turnabout, the scene of his first crime (the *Esperanca*) is about to return to him. He discovers that the letter he had written to Helen in which he wrecklessly expressed his attachment to her has disappeared without her having seen it, and that someone as a result now has some evidence which could be used in blackmailing him. When he gets home after the already shattering day, he is dismayed by the telegram from Louise informing him that she is on her way back.   As if to complete a cosmic conspiracy against him, a typhoon all at once blows up.   Pursued so relentlessly by his fate (and Greene sets up this process so that it almost seems foreordained), Scobie begins to think seriously about suicide.

That he hesitates at all is natural enough, for he believes in the church's teaching that it is the worst sin, even though he tries very hard to convince himself that Christ's crucifixion is a kind of precedent:

> The priests told you that it was the unforgivable sin, the
> final expression of an unrepentant despair, and of course
> one accepted the Church's teaching. But they taught also
> that God had sometimes broken his own laws, and was it
> more impossible for him to put out a hand of forgiveness
> into the suicidal darkness and chaos than to have woken

himself in the tomb, behind the stone? Christ had killed
himself (*HOM*, pp. 206-207).

Scobie is indeed pushing moral interpretations to sophistical ex-
tremes; but because he has a strong element of logic, he cannot
ultimately deceive himself.[26]

These thoughts indicate not so much his theological convictions as his psychological yearning for self-destruction. A dream
he has is particularly revealing of his growing awareness of his
decadence:

> That night he dreamed that he was in a boat drifting down
> just such an underground river as his boyhood hero Allan
> Quatermain had taken towards the lost city of Milosis.
> But Quatermain had companions, while he was alone, for
> you couldn't count the dead body on the stretcher as a
> companion. He felt a sense of urgency, for he told him-
> self that bodies in this climate kept for a very short time,
> and the smell of decay was already in his nostrils. Then,
> sitting there guiding the boat down the mid-stream, he
> realized that it was not the dead body that smelt but his
> own living one (*HOM*, p. 246).

Scobie imagines with horror that he has reached the point where
he is not only the cause of immense pain for Louise and Helen
but also for God. As he forsees the possibility of a future of
sacrilegious masses, he has a "picture before his eyes of a bleeding face, of eyes closed by the continuous shower of blows: the
punch-drunk head of God reeling sideways" (*HOM*, p. 264).
The final blow to God is, he imagines, the murder of Ali, his servant of fifteen years, through his complicity with Yusef because
of Scobie's unjust suspicion that Ali was capable of betrayal.
When he sees the body of Ali, he imagines that of God because
he has betrayed both even though he has also loved them. And
due to this shock of recognition, which barely averts a damning
sort of pride, he recovers the distinction between pity and love.

It is in this final context of love that we must look at
Scobie's suicide.[27] It becomes an act of atonement, not of escape or self-crucifixion. His last words—"Dear God, I love . . . "
—may seem at first ambiguous.[28] Yet they are ambiguous only
if one fails to see that he has undergone an afferent movement
from an abstract vision of cosmic pity in which "the heart of

the matter" is that one must "feel pity even for the planets" to a faith in the potency of divine love.

Greene has said that a suicide which is successful "is often only a cry for help which hasn't been heard in time."[29]   In Scobie's case God, at any rate, has heard. That God's love is present and receptive is suggested in several ways after Scobie has reached the suicidal point.   Scobie imagines that a mysterious "someone outside the room" was actually "seeking him" as he approaches his final minutes; the mysterious fingers and voice which try to hold him are those of grace.   As he falls to his death, the medal that was given to him by the grateful Portuguese captain strikes the floor and spins "like a coin under the ice-box—the saint whose name nobody could remember" (*HOM*, p. 299).   We know, of course, that Scobie will not be canonized; still, in his fall to grace he has experienced the agony of man's impotency and the power of God's love with the terrible intensity of a saint.   Significantly, it is God's vicar, Father Rank, who most cleary indicates the inscrutable nature of grace.   His answer to Louise's conviction that Scobie was surely damned is "don't imagine you—or I—know a thing about God's mercy" (*HOM*, p. 306).

When Greene started on *The Heart of the Matter*, it had been several years since he had actually written a novel due to his service in the Second World War.   Thus, as he would admit himself, he was a little rusty in his craft.[30]   This hardly ever becomes obvious mainly because, by this time, he had perfected the use of an ironic tone which could act consistently as a form of commentary while it also pulled the story together. Still, there are times when some of the descriptive and religiously weighted passages are clearly overloaded.   Moreover, by the end of the novel, there exists a feeling that the facets of the plot and the design of the theme have been controlled too carefully.   These problems, in turn, lead back to the fundamental one Greene had with this novel.   Significantly enough, this had to do with the question of point-of-view, something that Greene had apparently learned to master long ago.

When Greene settled on using the third person point-of-view for *The Heart of the Matter*, he was following the practice of all of his previous novels.   In all those books there is no reason to question Greene's choice.   But investing *The Heart of the Matter* with a point-of-view which, in his hands, gives almost total authority to Scobie's view of things led to an unforseen difficulty. Greene had actually set out to write a book whose central character would be a negative expression of the dangers of inordinate pride.[31] However, because we are made to see things from Scobie's perspective so completely, and because the line of the story is laid out in a somewhat rigid way, we eventually learn not only to trust him but to sympathize fully with him. This is why by the time we get to the words of Father Rank about God's grace we are obliged to feel that Scobie was surely not meant for damnation. Beyond that, we might feel that *The Heart of the Matter* is so schematic that perhaps Scobie was never really in danger because he wasn't free enough for us to have ever doubted his fate.

Taken as a whole, *The Heart of the Matter* is by no means a failure. In several ways it even represents some of Greene's best work. Green is, for example, often nothing less than brilliant in the way he manages to capture the African landscape as an authentic reflection of what he experienced while he was stationed there during the war and as a vivid metaphor for what was happening to the war-ravaged world. Moreover, this novel contains several of his most fully developed and striking characters. Yet because of his technical failure to create the kind of essential ambiguity he desired for this novel, Greene realized that he might have to change the strategy in the next novel he was planning in order to more effectively bring out the eschatological issues which would arise from it. Thus in *The End of the Affair*, the last of his Catholic tetralogy, he would finally try out an active first person narrator.[32] Of course, this approach would not lead to a flawless work. The main problem which Greene was aware of but which he could only partially resolve was the inherent nature of this approach to resist a narrative tone which had both variety and ambiguity. Yet largely because he challenged this paradoxical problem by going ahead with a change in his method, Greene would ultimately come up with a book which is at least more sympathetically involving than his previous Catholic novels.

The End of the Affair

If we consider the evidence presented in *Brighton Rock*, *The Power and the Glory*, and *The Heart of the Matter*, we are bound to agree with Mauriac that, up to this point in Greene's career, his primary subject had been "the hidden presence of God in an atheistic world."[33] In these books we are made to be aware that God is ever present, watching, apparently eager to answer if called upon, whispering the way to the lost. In *The End of the Affair* (1951), however, God takes a more explicit and active role. The result is the creation of an unusual drama in which an adulteress finds her way to sainthood and a skeptical and hate-ridden novelist gropes his way toward faith and a deeper comprehension of love.

There are elements in the story of Sarah Miles which make it resemble a conventional hagiography. Notably, her soul travels the path described by St. John as a necessarily nocturnal one in which "the point of departure is privation of all desire, and complete detachment from the world: the road is by faith, which is like night to the intellect; the goal, which is God, is incomprehensible while we are in this life."[34] Then, after her mystical union with God is complete, she is blessed with the gift of miracles. But such a reading would, of course, be far too simple. To begin with, Sarah's story also has some surprising and unorthodox twists and turns, starting with a highly provocative factor—the betrayal of her husband. Moreover, the story is told in such a way that the real focus finally turns on the first-person narrator, the hate-ridden novelist who eventually reveals his complex nature to himself and to us, but only after the involutions and ambiguities of his drama are put in order through careful analysis and judgment.

The catalyst of the story is the fact that between Sarah and Henry, her husband, exists a relationship which is devoid of passion. Because the most either can expect of the other is kindness, Sarah looks elsewhere to satisfy her intense longings for a more complete union. She appears to find the love she has been searching for in Bendrix, the novelist, and their affair does last for five years. Then Sarah suddenly ends it, and several months later she just as suddenly dies.

Soon thereafter—for cathartic, therapeutic, and professional reasons—Bendrix starts to write a novel about these events. He begins by describing an encounter with Henry which took place a number of months after the end of the affair. Henry is very disturbed by the growing suspicion that his wife is unfaithful to him because of her increasingly strange behavior. He wonders out loud whether he might not engage a private detective to investigate the possibility of adultery, but then he gives it up as an obscene thought. Bendrix, however, follows up the idea on his own initiative because he is consumed by jealousy. To his surprise, he comes to the realization that he has been replaced by God.

The process of Sarah's exchange of profane love for sacred love began the very day that marked the death of the illicit affair. That day Bendrix is surprised by the blast of one of the first V-1 rockets raining on war-time London. Sarah, finding him to all appearances dead, prays wildly: "Dear God . . . make me believe. I can't believe. Make me. . . . I'm a bitch and a fake and I hate myself. I can't do anything of myself. *Make* me believe. . . . Let him be alive, and I *will* believe. Give him a chance. Let him have his happiness. Do this, and I'll believe. But that wasn't enough. It doesn't hurt to believe. So I said, I love him and I'll do anything if You'll make him alive. I said very slowly, I'll give him up forever, only let him be alive with a chance. . . . "[35] And then Bendrix walked in. He believes that he has only been momentarily stunned by the explosion; she is convinced that her prayer has been answered. As a result she attempts to keep her desperate vow.

The ordeal to keep her part of the bargain with God (described, like all of Sarah's subjective facts, in her diary) is naturally painful. She finds that she is terribly lonely, particularly for Bendrix. Besides, there is the persisting temptation to rationalize away the existence of God. To be convinced of this wild hope, she goes to Smythe, a rationalist, for private discussions. Ironically, his arguments that God is only a chimera assure her to the contrary. Then, with belief comes the light of faith followed by a vision of divine love.

When Bendrix discovers that he has been jealous of a spiritual rival, he assumes that he can win Sarah back since he can offer her a love which is not abstract. He calls her on the telephone to insist that he is coming over immediately to take her with him once and for all; but he only succeeds in driving her out into the rain in a wild attempt to escape him. As a result, she catches pneumonia, and within a matter of days she dies. He is naturally embittered and stunned by the events. But it is the discovery that Sarah appears to be the source of a series of miracles that sends him into a terrible struggle with God. First there is what he would have preferred to see as the coincidence that his mock prayer to Sarah at her funeral to save him from becoming involved with a certain available young woman is answered. Then the touch of a relic of Sarah's hair seems to cure Smythe of a facial birthmark that was perhaps the source of his rebellion against God. And the son of Parkis, the detective who spied on Sarah for Bendrix, is cured of intense abdominal pains by what the boy says was a visitation by her in the night. What haunts Bendrix most, though, is Sarah's diary, which Parkis lifted during the course of his investigation and which now possesses Bendrix. Its presence in the hands of Bendrix seems to be assurance that the miracle of his cure from self-indulgent hatred will follow.

All this is told in a slightly disjointed way to reflect not only Bendrix's mental and emotional condition but also the fact that this story has professional consequences for him. Bendrix has been the author of several modestly successful novels in the past. There are some critics and loyal followers who admire his sense of style and his polished technique in particular. Greater success, though, has constantly eluded him because, as he comes to suspect, he has in fact been too finished and slick. He has had methodical control over his works, apparently to the extent that they had no life of their own. Now, however, he starts a story which from the very beginning threatens to progress on its own. His first sentence expresses his belief that he, as a novelist, arbitrarily selects where to begin and end a story; but his second sentence is already a statement of doubt. A few sentences later he declares that this will be a record of hatred; we soon realize, however, that the story will be transformed into a record of love. As he begins, he thinks that if he is writing against the grain of his prejudices he has nothing to fear since his professional pride will encourage him to tell the truth, or at least the near truth. Nevertheless, what becomes most fearful to him is actually his realization that he does not even know the truth about himself and that his story is known in its entirety and can only be told by God. After he comes to the realization that God has replaced him not only as the lover of Sarah but also as the writer of his novel, he tries to resist by expressing his hatred. However, since grace has an active interest in Bendrix, his determination to be an outrage to God is futile. In fact, by trying to deny divine prerogative Bendrix assures his fate, since in Greene's religious world grace seeks out the rebels because by their actions they probe the mystery of God.[36] Besides, as Greene has pointed out about his various sinners, Bendrix might try to sin against God but he does not manage to do so very successfully.[37] His rebellious words actually indicate that he is going through a stage of mental suffering and terror, and in Greene's fiction this is a necessary prelude to spiritual transformation. When the mortal terror becomes unbearable, so does the temptation to surrender to divine power. In a sense, one might say that the book finally develops into a testament of the irresistible nature of grace. Greene has described that faith originally came to him formless but with overwhelming certainty. The apocalypse Bendrix finally experiences is even more disembodied but just as absolute.

If Bendrix's spiritual journey is more prolonged than Sarah's, it is mainly because he is possessed by pride. Sarah's sins are all of the flesh, and hence there is no serious obstacle to her reaching the stage of heroic virtue. Bendrix's sins, however, are of the mind and consequently are much more insidious. His intellectual pride as a novelist allows him to delve into the lives of others with detachment, yet ultimately not with impunity. Since pride is self-devouring, the final consquence is emotional sterility. Fortunately for Bendrix, he is allowed soon after he starts his book to realize that he has really become deficient both in hatred and love. When he finally does recognize his insufficiency, he is taking the characteristically Christian first step toward the possibility of redemption. With humility comes the acceptance of guilt, and with guilt the yearning to confess. That his proposed novel actually becomes a spiritual diary and confession is by now clear, and what is also clear to the reader though not to Bendrix is that it becomes an exemplum of Christian love. We can recognize that Sarah's love imitates the passion of Christ. But we also come to the understanding before Bendrix does that he is entering the territory of Christian love in his growing affection for Parkis, Henry, and Sarah. Since selfless love is strange to Bendrix, he is naturally apprehensive. More frightening to him, though, is the realization of what must surely follow if he gives up his hatred for God. After reading once again the final page of Sarah's diary in which she prays to God to give him peace, Bendrix reveals the depth of his dread of submitting to the divine mystery:

> What I chiefly felt was less hate than fear. For if this God exists, I thought, and if even you—with your lusts and your adulteries and the timid lies you used to tell—can change like this, we could all be saints by leaping as you

> leapt, by shutting the eyes and leaping once and for all;
> if *you* are a saint, it's not so difficult to be a saint. It's
> something He can demand of any of us—leap! But I won't
> leap (*EOA,* p. 209).

These words of panic, part of the highly charged final scene of
the book, are, of course, chiefly ironic. Bendrix is not about to
become a saint, but he is on the verge of taking the fearful leap.
Exhausted by the relentless pursuit of grace, he glances at the distance he has already traveled and expresses his surrender in
quietly ironic terms in the final paragraph:

> I wrote at the start that this was a record of hate, and,
> walking there beside Henry . . . I found the one prayer
> that seemed to serve the winter mood: O God, You've
> done enough, You've robbed me of enough. I'm too tired
> and old to learn to love. Leave me alone forever (*EOA,*
> p. 211).

In tracing Bendrix's path to this point of reluctant salvation, Greene exhibits a notable extension of his art. Having combined the subjective narrative method with a kind of novel-
within-a-novel approach, he succeeds in creating a story which
contains more structural complexity, emotional resonance, and
purposeful ambiguity than any of his previous books. At the
same time, it must be said that this book has less of that urgent
passion which gives so much power to his previous religious
novels. This, paradoxically, seems connected with the fact that
there are some things about *The End of the Affair* which ultimately suggest Greene had now perhaps gone further as a writer
than he might have meant to in the area of religious abstractions,
and that it was therefore inevitable this would be his last pointed-
ly Catholic book.

The End of the Catholic Cycle

In taking Greene's Catholic novels together, it becomes clear
that they can be read as a remarkable tetralogy on the subject
of grace. One might go so far as to call these books comedies of
salvation, since in each of them the protagonist travels through

ever widening spheres of infernal terror until he finally emerges into the territory of grace. The progress of each of these characters has unique factors, but a general examination of their spiritual journeys shows us their forms are essentially the same. That Greene begins in *medias res* serves to dramatize the fact the protagonists are all initially suspended between the saving power of grace and the fatal attraction of evil, between heaven and hell. While in this state of suspension, their suffering is dreadful as the supernatural struggle for their souls rages. Their having the imagination to recognize what is at stake while experiencing the relentless tension of the opposing forces is actually the first indication they are not doomed. With the conviction of the reality of heaven and hell, Greene indicates, one is saved from amoral sterility; and with the experience of deep suffering, particularly after one becomes involved with others who also suffer, one is led to the conviction that pain and evil are the way of life. Greene follows the view of St. Augustine in suggesting that this recognition of the ineluctable reality of evil is the first clear concession to the force of grace.[38] What constantly pulls in the opposite direction, though, is pride, since it is the source of that deceptive feeling of self-sufficiency. This is why a shattering experience of failure precedes the ultimate leap to faith. Failure makes one aware of his insignificance when placed against the backdrop of the supernatural dimension, and it also allows one to identify himself with the myth of fallen man. When one has reached the point where he can feel such a sense of rare humility, he is near to attaining that understanding of himself and his spiritual destiny Greene calls the "religious sense."[39] If he then gives himself up to divine judgment, he will discover that the more dreadful his failures, the greater the appalling mercy of God.

If it's obvious that these novels are thoroughly informed with the spirit of Catholic doctrine, in the end they actually offer a personal mythology. Perhaps it is true to say that Greene, feeling deprived of an inherited or unbroken tradition of Christianity, had finally to invent a system of his own in the manner of such other modern writers as Lawrence, Pound, and Yeats.[40] This is not to suggest that there is anything dishonest about his declared religion; yet there is no doubt that Greene's Catholicism is unorthodox. Above all, Greene's view of the mercy of God is distinctive. As we have seen, he assumes that the mystery of God's grace is so great there are no formal religious rules which can comprehend it, and that instead the patterns and means of theological salvation are as strange as sacred love. Greene's quest is not to try to uncover that mystery of God. Instead, as one critic puts it, he moves "stealthily deeper into the darkness, moves through the annihilation of our confidence in human knowledge to an awareness of impenetrable mystery, moves from the deceptive light to the queerly nourishing obscurity. All the truth of things, for Greene, lies hidden in the darkness. . . ."[41] That one can never reach the heart of this darkness may be a terrifying fact in Greene's religious novels; paradoxically, though, it's also presented as the source of animating faith.

There are very few novelists who have so compellingly employed the techniques of realism and melodrama to investigate religious themes. Thus it was a surprise to many of Greene's admirers when he declared after writing *The End of the Affair* that his next novel would not be concerned with explicitly Catholic themes.[42] Why Greene made such a decision is naturally intriguing. Had he perhaps become a burnt-out Catholic? There were those critics who guessed this was the case, and that Bendrix's final prayer moreover implied that religion as a creative spring had now simply run dry for Greene.[43] At this point in Greene's career, however, such a conclusion was at least premature and exaggerated. The actual fact seems to be that Greene stopped writing Catholic novels after his fourth one not because he was then losing his religion but because he had been led so far by his religious considerations in general and the theme of grace in particular that he felt his art threatened.

Greene has made the standard disclaimer that his characters should not be mistaken for their author. Neverthless, after reading *The End of the Affair* one comes away with the strong impression that the alarming situation of Bendrix is at least to some extent symptomatic of the state of Greene's mind. There appears no doubt that Bendrix's soul will be saved; but what about his art? As Bendrix prepares for the religious leap, he reveals that he is ready to reject the validity not only of reason and consciousness but also of the aesthetic approach to life.[44] The implications of his climactic frame of mind are extensive, going so far in fact as to suggest that Bendrix could not indeed be saved without giving up his intellectual vocation. At this point one might begin to wonder if Greene does not appear to show that art, which is the product of ego, is not mutually exclusive from faith, with follows the surrender of ego. In making the reluctant

Bendrix a captive of the irresistible force of grace, Greene leaves the impression that spiritual determinism is the explanation for both what happens and what is written. Bendrix's story ends up differently from his original intention not because he has become indecisive in his work but because God is the master artist who conditions his vicar novelist.[45] Greene has agreed with the view that in *The End of the Affair* he has written "a novel about plot making . . . not only about a novelist making a plot, but about God making a plot."[46] Significantly, he has also made the statement in referring to the introduction of the miracles without natural explanations that he had "made an appalling mistake. . . ."[47] Consequently, we have an implicit paradox here that is disturbing. Who is responsible for those "mistakes," as the book was written, Bendrix, Greene, or God? One wonders where Greene meant to draw the line between God's province and the province of his own artistic imagination. In describing his state of mind as he approached his conversion to Catholicism, Greene has indicated that he had earlier feared the possibility there was no such dividing line at all.[48] Eventually this issue would cease to bother Greene. At that point in his career, however, he was still devout enough in his religion to be troubled deeply by this dilemma.

The fact that Greene's Catholic novels didn't clearly resolve the issue of spiritual determinism is what was behind a minor critical war. Because these novels are so dominated by the theme of God's mercy, various critics became occupied with trying to interpret Greene's precise understanding of evil and grace. Thus John Atkins, for example, is convinced that what Greene had written about the presence of evil in the works of Dickens is really true of his own novels: "the eternal and alluring taint of the Manichee, with its simple and terrible explanation of our plight, how the world was made by Satan and not by God, lulling us with the music of despair. . . ."[49] Sean O'Faolin concludes that Greene is clearly writing in the tradition of Pascal and Jansenism.[50] Francis Kunkel is not so sure, for he is bothered by an occasional theological paradox: "To believe, as Greene obviously does, that some characters are forever outside the pale of grace and so incapable of religious belief and experience is to cast a gratuitous slur on God's mercy and to flirt with Jansenism. Greene's position here is inconsistent because ordinarily he follows Pascal in setting no limits to God's mercy."[51] Refining his interpretation, he concludes that Greene is not Pelagian nor

completely Manichaean, but half Manichaean.[52] It is no wonder
that the drift toward theological esoterica by his critics eventually prompted a complaint from Greene:

> People who think they are getting at Jansenism in my
> novels usually do not know what Jansenism really means.
> They probably mean Manichaenism. This is because in
> the Catholic novels I seem to believe in a supernatural
> evil. One gets so tired of people saying that my novels
> are about the opposition of Good and Evil. They are not
> about Good and Evil, but about human beings.[53]

Despite Greene's objection, however, one is prone to come
away from these religious novels with the feeling he has been a
witness to dramas less human than divine. This is due primarily
to their conclusions. These novels slide rather conspicuously
from realism to abstract didacticism as they approach the end. As
a consequence, one is bound to agree with a view of David Pryce-
Jones that because "finally nothing in the novels seems to derive
from human vagary, there is a discrepancy between the involved
world which Greene sets out to portray in all its complications
and the rigid solutions he imposes at the end."[54] And as Morton
Dauwen Zabel in particular has pointed out, the drift in these
novels toward explicitly theological conclusions has unfortunate
artistic consequences. He suggests that

> the fiction that embodies such arguments soon runs into
> the difficulty which all tendentious or didactic fiction
> sooner or later encounters. It no longer "argues" the
> problems and complexities or character in terms of psy-
> chological and moral forces; it states, decides, and solves
> them in terms of pre-established and dictated premises.
> Grace is always held in reserve as a principle of salva-
> tion. . . . Greene . . . shirks nothing in presenting his men
> and women as psychically complex and morally con-
> founded. But as he advances out of parable into realism,
> out of the tale of violence into the drama of credible
> human personalities, he still keeps an ace up his sleeve,
> and grace is called upon to do the work that normally
> would be assigned to moral logic and nemesis.[55]

Needless to say, it is debatable just how much Greene might

have been influenced by such criticism into deciding to write novels with different forms and perspectives. There seems no doubt, however, that because of his venturesome temperament he experienced increasing impatience and frustration with what had become something of a formula. Beyond that, it's easy to imagine this peripatetic writer simply deciding to compose novels which did not explicitly focus on the subject of religious salvation because of a restless ambition to explore new regions. He had surveyed the territory of grace; the map was as complete as the imagination would allow. What lay beyond was also absorbing. In explaining how he came to choose his subjects, Greene once said: "What it really adds up to is that I write novels about what interests me and I can't write about anything else. And one of the things which interests me most is discovering the humanity in the apparently inhuman character."[56] We have seen that the protagonists of the Catholic cycle reveal their humanity primarily in their struggles with supernatural forces, most obviously with grace. In the novels which follow *The End of the Affair,* however, one can recognize a shift in emphasis and direction, with the dramatized conflicts of the protagonists now clearly presented in less abstract, more secular terms.

Beginning with the publication of *The Quiet American* in 1955, Greene is seen to explore the problem of what man himself can do to salvage something meaningful and worthwhile from the here and now.[57] This shift is not an extreme one, it should be stressed. Greene's techniques and obsessions remain essentially the same. Even the protagonists are reminiscent in many ways of their predecessors. Bendrix in particular seems to be their model, but with important differences. He is saved from withering hatred and cynicism by the intervention of a divine energy. The protagonists who follow Bendrix, however, are increasingly less confounded by the divine challenge and are progressively more involved with the insistent demands of the social, political, and human spheres.[58] They might be faced with a variety of difficult moral problems, too; but their decisive acts finally depend not on theological dogma but on secular considerations. If faith is still the operative term, it is now used in a more personal and existential sense. In this regard, the critic Stanford Sternlicht is quite correct in his claim that Greene's hope now begins to reside "not only nor primarily in after life, but in the distinctly encouraging possibility of living in dignity during this worldly existence."[59] Yet he is not wholly accurate when he goes on to say that what saves these later protagonists from corrosive despair is a belief in some system.[60]   Their actual means of liberation turns out to be less abstract and surprisingly conspicuous.   In the Catholic novels the apparently doomed characters can find their way to God through a radical experience of spiritual immolation.   In the subsequent novels, though, the protagonists must, as a rule, venture through the treacherous maze of egoism to the point where they come upon the discovery that what can save them is the resolution to become engaged in the hazards of human affection.

IV

THE QUIET AMERICAN: A SECULAR PROSPECT

When Greene wrote *The Quite American* (1955), he was as fully in command of his craft as he would ever be. In fact, it can be argued that this novel is actually his most flawlessly wrought. It's particularly notable that Greene now manages to avoid the descriptive and metaphorical excesses which occasionally appear in his earlier works, and his use of the first person narrative approach fits in more perfectly with his structural and thematic concerns than it did in *The End of the Affair.* Nevertheless, *The Quiet American* has always been his most controversial and widely misunderstood book. No doubt, that's partly due to the fact that many of his readers weren't prepared to shift from his Catholic themes toward a secular direction. But there is another, more insistent, reason for the misinterpretations. Many people have misread or downright objected to the novel on the grounds of what they felt were its biased political assumptions. Not surprisingly, this has been especially the case in the United States. When the book first appeared in this country, it was immediately met with a great deal of hostility. Critics left and right charged Greene with having essentially written a petulant tract against Americans and their ambitions in world affairs, particularly in Indochina. Once the Vietnamese war became a fact, and the political commentary in the book was found to have been incisive and prophetic to an astonishing degree, it began winning more and more praise from critics here as well as abroad. However, this new reputation which the novel is enjoying is largely based on an unsound impression which continues to persist, that the book is meant to be primarily read as an anti-war story.[1] It should be made clear, though, that although war and politics are prominent issues in the novel, they serve to poise the ultimate concern of personal salvation.

This issue of personal salvation is concentrated primarily in the character of Fowler, the narrator of the book, and in the way he tells his story. Even the anti-American element which aroused so much criticism when the novel was first published must be seen now as having more to do with the fate of Fowler than with that of the world at large. In other words, Fowler's expressions of contempt for all things American are less symptomatic of his politics than of his intellectual and emotional condition. As a political reporter of long experience, he has come to look upon the United States as the force which carries the most responsibility for the misery of the world because it happens to be the greatest power. To his mind, the United States has actually become the symbol of what was wrong with modern civilization. These views, through their extreme logic, can suggest the mind of an idealist and a cynic, perhaps in a state of serious conflict. If he holds a grudge against Americans it is because of one particular American. It is Pyle, the "quiet American," who arrives on the scene in Vietnam to liberate Fowler from his emotional and spiritual exhaustion. But Pyle is an unconscious, and paradoxical, savior. He enters Fowler's life suddenly to steal his girl and then to cause more misery in general by getting involved in terrorism. After Fowler witnesses a bombing caused by Pyle, he decides that his rival must be destroyed for the good of all. Thus when a political enemy of Pyle insinuates to Fowler the opportunity to fulfill his wish even though some violence might be involved, he gives in to temptation. After the death of the American, however, Fowler finds himself possessed by sorrow and guilt, the first real signs that he could be headed for a spiritual recovery.

Before Pyle's arrival, Fowler tried to feel satisfied with what life then offered—a loyal mistress, a quiet home, one day flowing into the next. But actually he is even then haunted by deep fears. He is terrorized by life, since it means suffering, and so he has tried to withdraw from it. Instead, his unnatural isolation has resulted in a kind of personal inferno reflected by the hellish setting in which he finds himself.

As is usual in Greene, the setting of *The Quiet American* is exotic, primitive, and violent.[2] Greene's detractors, who like to refer to his chosen settings as Greeneland, may wish to believe that his primary motive is sensationalism and melodrama. Obviously, though, there is a better reason. When he selects a tropical setting, he shows nature as sluggish and decaying but still energetic and impressive enough "to show up the forces of civilization as degenerate, makeshift and ugly."[3] If the scene is urban, it is often filled with images of industrial decadence reminiscent of

Eliot's wasteland. The controlling factor of the setting, whether tropical or urban, is seediness. Seediness is ubiquitous because, as Greene sees it, the experience of modern man is filled with rot and squalor. Seediness is a sign of our maladjustment and the deterioration of our civilization. Thus there is in Greene the pull to primitivism, to go back to a time which was chaste in order to begin again. The presence of violence is important because it is the one pure emotion that joins the primitive with the modern world. Unfortunately, the ontology of violence has been debased to the point where it now expresses most urgently the horror of the present century. The setting of a Greene novel, then, functions as an important symbol of the civilization which has created it.

In a less direct way, the setting also functions to make clear the predicaments of the various characters. In *The Quiet American* the political hell of Vietnam serves especially to reflect and dramatize the inner state of Fowler. Vietnam is a land filled with horror. There is the ever-present danger of sudden death, whether in a contested military area or in a public square. If one loses a leg because of a bicycle bomb, it is considered as merely a poor joke. In *The Heart of the Matter* ubiquitous carrion birds hover over the failure and approaching death of Scobie. Here the birds are planes which do not wait for decay to set in; anything that moves is fair game. The flotsam of victims is everywhere, as omnipresent as the junk of war piling up. Knowing all this, Fowler, after he goes to a romantic movie with a happy ending, remarks that if it had been meant for children, "the sight of Oedipus emerging with his bleeding eyeballs from the palace at Thebes would surely give a better training for life today."[4] It is no wonder that Fowler is filled with cynicism, anxiety, and a terror of life, and that he consequently wishes to withdraw from it into a state of quiescence.

The title of the novel is actually ironic, for although Pyle is verbally quiet he is explosive in every other sense. It is Fowler who wishes so desperately for peace and who tries to insist that he is not involved:

> It had been an article of my creed. The human condition being what it was, let them fight, let them love, let them murder, I would not be involved. My fellow journalists called themselves correspondents; I preferred the title of reporter. I wrote what I saw: I took no action—even an opinion is a kind of action (*QA*, p. 23).

As it turns out, though, his wish for a life of radical detachment is futile. He finds out that he cannot really escape just by deciding to withdraw; events and people behind them will always interfere. Because he has a conscience, it will not allow him to rest when he is surrounded by pain. And he discovers that his chosen world of isolation is actually a kind of hell in itself which causes a torturous sense of alienation and a profound malaise which are akin to a living death.

Fowler is an opium smoker, for this drug can dull the pains of conscience for a time and abstract the spectacle of human misery. Eventually, of course, it can lead to the point where life is no longer a torture because it has become insubstantial. But a concomitant result is that the heart is in atrophy. In concrete terms, one will finally become like Mr. Chou: "with the indifferent gaze of a smoker; the sunken cheeks, the baby wrists, the arms of a small girl—many years and many pipes had been needed to whittle him down to these dimensions" (*QA*, p. 139). Human dignity is reduced to an "extreme emaciation" resembling a "piece of grease-proof paper that divides the biscuits in a tin" (*QA*, p. 138). In the back of his mind Fowler realizes that Mr. Chou represents himself as he might be, a part of the wreckage which surrounds the ancient opium smoker and which at the same time represents in real terms the accomplishments of that life.

In the course of the story Fowler goes through a process of psychological and spiritual regeneration, but the way is elaborate and agonizing. We can follow this process, however, by analyzing the narrative form, the structure of the story, and the persons whom Fowler encounters.

In *The Quiet American* Greene employs the basic form of the detective story. This is not surprising, since by now Greene was naturally predisposed to the genre. The reasons for this have everything to do with the nature of his art. The aesthetic and thematic conventions of this genre tend to embrace a number of the obsessions which have personally haunted him and which he has continuously wished to investigate. Of these, terror, guilt, violence, betrayal, and mystery are the most prevalent. The detective story's most obvious element of pursuit also creates the most interest through suspense; but this element has a symbolic function as well. It serves to dramatize the emotional condition of being on the run and is an appropriate "analogue of our search for the way out of confusion."[5] To Greene, the detective story is a modern fairy tale which perhaps is most effective in expressing the outrageous truth about the twentieth century, that it is a slide into savagery.   In effect, he prefers this genre because it can serve best to illustrate our times, and Greene's ultimate interest is always the means of arriving at precise truth.[6]   By pursuing and ferreting out truth, he believes, life at least becomes less inane if not necessarily less painful.

The protagonist in *The Quiet American* goes through just such a process.   He is the detective who follows the clues which lead him to the truth.   Needless to say, this is no ordinary who-done-it.   The twist is that the clues of guilt lead the pursuer to himself.   At the end of the investigation Fowler discovers that he is guilty of the crime.   Moreover, in a cunning turn-about, he finds as he follows the personal leads of alienation, malaise, guilt, and finally responsibility that the someone he had believed dead was still alive.   That is, at the vortex of the mystery he finds himself.

A conventional element of the detective thriller is the confession at the end. *The Quiet American,* though, goes further because the whole story is in the form of a dramatic confession.   But if Fowler has the desire to confess, does anyone really listen?   Is it, as one critic suggests, only a frustrated confession?[7]   In Greene's Catholic novels there are the surrogates of God to perform this function, and ultimately God himself listens.   Yet if Fowler's last words possibly indicate the wish that there were a God to whom he could apologize for his life, it is still only a wish, although such a hope might eventually turn out to be the first step toward a religious faith.   Whether or not Fowler will finally take a leap to God remains only speculation in the context of the novel; at the time of his final words of confession his vision of life is still clearly secular.   Hence it is appropriate that his confession as a whole be directed at the secular parallel of a priest, a policeman who represents political instead of divine power.   Vigot is, however, a silent confessor who does not appear to have much success in his efforts, because Fowler never tells him directly his whole story of involvement with the American whose death the policeman is responsible for investigating.   That Vigot does not succeed in getting a direct confession is not really important, though; the important point is that Fowler has the compulsion to admit the truth, however painful the process may be.   Without knowing it, Vigot actually does force Fowler to continue to reconstruct his story at least for his own analysis, purgation, and atonement after each meeting that the two have until the facts are all in and Fowler can lift his full burden of responsibility.

It is not true that Fowler, as one critic calls him, is an "obtuse narrator."[8] His problem is that he is afraid of what he does know. He is understandably relucatant to reconstruct his story because what waits at the end is something which might destroy his present hold on life. The danger awaiting him as he travels through the jungle of self-discovery is the realization that he has been involved in a murder and that perhaps he will never be able to be uninvolved again.

To dramatize the terror of Fowler and to reflect the analytical, convoluted self-exploration of his haunted mind as it hunts down the clues which will explain its emotional state, the structure of Greene's novel is purposely fragmented. At first one does make the observation that the grand aesthetic structure of the book is quite neat. Like a well-made play, the story falls naturally into the four parts that divide it, with each part organized around a central event. Thus in Part I Fowler meets Pyle. In Part II his life is saved by Pyle. But in Part III the American steals Fowler's girl away and shocks him with the discovery that Pyle has been responsible for a terrorist explosion which kills and maims the innocent and young. Consequently, in Part IV Fowler sees to it that the American is killed. These parts follow each other with relentless logic to an anticipated end; that is, if this were merely a simple story of revenge.

Within the neat exterior frame, the structure, just like Fowler, is complicated. In the first chapter of the novel we find out that the "quiet American" is dead, but it is difficult to suspect Fowler of any direct involvement. We are led to believe that at the very start of the story he is only waiting for Pyle, who has been delayed for some unexplained reason. One cannot know at the time that when Fowler says he wishes he were Pyle he is wishing for death. One is prone to accept Fowler's remark which ends the chapter at face value: "Am I the only one who really cared for Pyle" (*QA*, p. 16)? On the other hand, there are disturbing signs that seem to indicate Fowler is not after all so innocent despite his repeated disclaimers to himself after he finds out about the death. Why does he repeat his claim of innocence, one has to ask, and why to himself? The answer, of course, is that this is an indication he will be the hardest one to convince he is not guilty. Since such thoughts are painful, he smokes opium, which allows him to drift into abstract thoughts of the meaning of Phuong, who "was a certain hour of the night and the promise of rest," and of Pyle, who "had diminished after several pipes" (*QA,* p. 4). But the escape from the ghost of Pyle and the questioning silence of Vigot is only temporary.

In the first scene of Chapter II we are suddenly transported back to the day when Fowler first met Pyle. In the second scene of the same chapter we are jerked back in time and then forward to the morning after Pyle's death when Fowler goes to the American's apartment in order to help Phuong retrieve her things. There he encounters Vigot again, and thus his mind is once more possessed by thoughts of guilt and involvement. In the next chapter we are again jerked back into the past, to the time when, two months after his arrival, Pyle was first introduced to Phuong by Fowler. The remainder of Part I then more or less stabilizes into a chronological sequence of events. Significantly, this orderly pattern continues throughout Part II, as if Fowler were more willing to face time because his mind was under the illusion of greater safety as the crime receded into the past.

Part III begins on a day some two weeks after Pyle's death with another meeting between Fowler and Vigot. Consequently, as we have noted before, Fowler's conscience once again is forced to take up the thread of the story which in the end constitutes a tortured confession, and the agony which is growing in the confessor is again suggested by the inner structure of the book. As the panic of the narrator grows, so does the division of scenes into smaller and more confined units, as if to reflect the narrower bounds of escape. Part I was divided into comparatively large, rather leisurely units of five chapters, each of which in turn was sub-divided into no more than two scenes. Fowler is far from fully confronting his guilt at this stage. But in Part II we find only three chapters, and the central one is divided into four scenes. It is in this central chapter that Fowler recalls the night he and Pyle spent together talking about religion, politics, and sex; so this is when they actually learned to know each other. Even more disturbing to Fowler's submerged conscience, it was during this night that Pyle saved his life. And now in Part III, where Fowler is approaching the critical point in the story at which he becomes involved in the death of the American, the first chapter is broken into five sections, as if to suggest a delaying tactic against the onrush of truth and to reflect a growing hysteria through its jerky structure.

Part IV opens with Fowler's mind once more going back to a meeting which is described at the beginning of Part III. This final encounter with Vigot spurs Fowler into completing his story. Having by now passed the crisis of facing his guilt, he has ceased to resist and is prepared to finish his confession. Again, the structure of the novel functions to reveal his state of mind. In this part we discover that the inner structure has a numerical symmetry. Chapter I has a scene in which Fowler faces his confessor for the last time. Chapter II is divided into three scenes in which he, respectively, re-lives being at the explosion which shocked him into taking action against Pyle, going to Heng to see what could be done to stop the American, and finally taking the irretrievable step of entering into a conspiracy of murder. The last chapter of the book follows only a quarter of an hour after Vigot has left, as if to tell us that Fowler is now more at peace with time. In its only scene Fowler can finally make his apology for his past guilt.

Once we have analyzed the structure and start to look at the story in its time sequence, we can also begin to recognize that, like the priest in *The Power and the Glory,* Fowler is a fugitive not so much from the forces of law as from the terrifying knowledge that awaits him. He is a secular traveler, of course, and thus he will surrender to the immaterial force which pursues him more reluctantly. Nevertheless, like the priest, he is not only a geographical but also a mental itenerant who continually comes upon people who function as haunting images of his various sides and lead to a full self-knowledge.

We have already seen that Mr. Chou, the opium addict, serves to suggest to Fowler a grotesquerie of the man who withdraws from life. And we have also already seen that Vigot functions as a reflection of Fowler's conscience and an exorcist of his poisonous guilt. The reason why Vigot is so effective, though, is in itself revealing. When we first see Vigot, he too might appear to represent a man who has withdrawn from life because of "his weariness with . . . the whole human condition" (*QA,* p. 9). Yet although Vigot is weary, he is still interested enough to read Pascal and to wonder about the fate of humanity. He pursues Fowler not merely out of a sense of duty but because he has become involved in the quest for truth and in Fowler's destiny. Fowler is struck by the fact that Vigot after one of their meetings "had looked at me with compassion, as he might have looked at some prisoner for whose capture he was responsible undergoing his sentence for life" (*QA,* p. 154). Fowler has some legitimate fear of the law at this time; however, as he comes to understand, what Vigot's look ultimately meant was that he was aware of the fact that we are all serving life-sentences of a sort. As he had earlier told Fowler, in life one does not have the choice to wager once he has embarked, and that consequently Fowler was "*engagé,* like the rest of us" (*QA,* p. 152).

The last meeting with Vigot is particularly revealing of the detective's effect upon the mind of Fowler. After Vigot leaves, Fowler is astonished at how much he has been disturbed by failing to verbally express his guilt to him: "It was as though a poet had brought me his work to criticize and through some careless action I had destroyed it. I was a man without a vocation . . . but I could recognize a vocation in another" (*QA,* p. 190). Vigot's having a true vocation, which causes him to be embroiled in the mire of humanity, is what gives Fowler "the feeling of some force immobile and profound" (*QA,* p. 189). As Fowler realizes, Vigot "would have made a good priest" because it was "so easy to confess" to someone who is "sympathetically involved instead of shocked by humanity" (*QA,* p. 186). Moreover, Fowler is drawn to Vigot because of the latter's comprehension of the desires and motives of a confessor—to purge oneself, to rest from deception, and to see oneself clearly. Fowler, of course, feels a need for purgation and truth, and above all for self-knowledge.

When Fowler originally came to the Orient, it was for a different purpose than self-discovery. What he desired more than anything was peace, and he thought he could find it by escaping from himself. He had been married, had had affairs, and they each ended in disaster. Because he had been terrified of the end of love, he had rushed toward the finish "just like a coward runs towards the enemy and wins a medal"; in each case he "wanted to get death over" (*QA,* p. 111). In the East he again begins an affair; but because he believes that Phuong, as the myth about Oriental women goes, is a creature of loyalty instead of love, he has the illusion of safety. He feels certain that love is no real threat in this affair because of his pre-conception of Phuong that he describes to Pyle:

> It's a cliche to call them children—but there's one thing which is childish. They love you in return for kindness,

> security, the presents you give them—they hate you for
> a blow or an injustice. They don't know what it's like—
> just walking into a room and loving a stranger. For an
> aging man . . . it's very secure . . . (*QA*, p. 112).

Fowler may deny it, but at first he is a Berkeleyan in his attitude toward Phuong. He has abstracted her into a symbol. To him she is not an independent creature who is capable of surprising acts and feelings; she is only an ambience or emotion, "invisible like peace" (*QA*, p. 43). Only with his growing self-knowledge does he finally come to understand that he "was inventing a character" and that for all one "could tell, she was as scared as the rest of us: she didn't have the gift of expression, that was all" (*QA*, p. 147). What he is discovering is that if Phuong was capable of fear and terror, then she had exhibited a remarkable quality of endurance. Consequently, even though in the beginning of this story Fowler denies that Phuong's name, which means phoenix, applies to her in any symbolic way since "nothing nowadays is fabulous, and nothing rises from its ashes" (*QA*, p. 3), it is precisely her genius for renewal which ultimately beguiles him, because he is seized by a suppressed but powerful yearning for such an experience.

After Phuong leaves him for Pyle, Fowler flies north to report on the war and to get away from the spectre of self-pity. There he meets Trouin, a young French pilot who has the wisdom which is usually the result of many years. Trouin takes Fowler up for a bombing run, and nothing particularly out of the ordinary happens during it. On the return flight, however, Trouin quite suddenly blasts a harmless looking sampan apart. Fowler is shaken, as he describes it, by the abrupt "fortuitous choice of a prey—we had just happened to be passing; one burst only was required; there was no one to return fire; we were gone again, adding our little quota to the world's dead" (*QA*, p. 167). Only that night when Trouin takes him to an opium house does Fowler learn about the pilot's deep and painful remorse. Angrily, he exclaims to Fowler and the world which seemed not to understand: "I'm not fighting a colonial war. Do you think I'd do these things for the planters of Terre Rouge? I'd rather be court-martialled. We are fighting all of your wars, but you leave us the guilt" (*QA*, p. 168). Refusing to dismiss his crimes on professional grounds, Trouin is a victim of his conscience who is willing to carry his guilt about with him. That he does join a quality of compassion with a sense of responsible objectivity is a source of continuing agony for him but is at the same time what saves his humanity.

Trouin's weight of guilt is religious in nature, since he accepts it as a necessary part of human limitations. One cannot remain innocent, detached, and yet human too. As he says at one point in answer to Fowler's declaration of non-involvement: "It's not a matter of reason or justice. We all get involved in a moment of emotion, and then we cannot get out. War and Love—they have always been compared. . . . I would not have it otherwise" (*QA*, p. 168). This train of thought has truly arrived at the heart of Fowler's moral turmoil, so that later that night he finds himself impotent to enter into the body of a beautiful prostitute because, he realizes, "the ghost of what I'd lost proved more powerful than the body stretched at my disposal" (*QA*, p. 170). The thought of Phuong is one ghost; but the memories of his lost humanity aroused by Trouin are also haunting him.

Trouin, of course, is not the only one who suggests to Fowler that he cannot choose not to be engaged without losing his soul. Such admonitions, in fact, become a dominant counterpoint to the theme of despair in what amounts to a kind of confessional fugue. We have already seen that Vigot was properly the one to commence the refrain of commitment. The letter Fowler receives from his wife in which she refuses to grant him a divorce sounds the same note. And Mr. Heng, who represents the Communist forces which are eager to be rid of Pyle, sums it up most directly: "Sooner or later . . . one has to take sides. If one is to remain human" (*QA*, p. 194).

Fowler finally accepts the view of this statement, but only after struggling against and experiencing its disquieting consequences. And it is predominantly his relationship with Pyle that makes the truth of it come home to stay, for Pyle in the end functions as an opposing reflection which discloses his true self and as his moral incubus.

Fowler and Pyle are so delineated as to suggest on one level of interpretation a dramatic antagonism between characters of antithetical positions, between realism and romanticism, experience and innocence, and between detachment and commitment.[9] This pattern of oppositions serves at first to make more concrete the characters of the two and to create the drama of a clash of characters. But ultimately this technique points to the

more important issues of how the extreme positions of both represent failure and how a mature synthesis is necessary.[10] If
this structure of opposition were used to isolate the factual evidence of Pyle's effect on Fowler, then it would appear that
Greene is skirting mere melodrama. Fowler's involvement in
the death of Pyle, however, does not just get rid of a dangerous
rival in love. It is an act which shakes him out of a tired com-
placency and into guilt.[11] Moreover, on a symbolic level, it
forces him into the realization that he had been responsible for
killing his savior.

Pyle saves Fowler once from a violent death; but what the
American does not know is that he saves Fowler in a spiritual
way, too. At the end of Part I there is an evocative allusion to
Dante's *Purgatorio*. This reference is appropriate in one sense,
at least, because Fowler is truly wandering through circles of
infernal despair. Ironically, he is led out of this region by Pyle,
who actually does not know where he is going himself since he
is blinded by the false light of his political idealism. But a dream
which Fowler has suggests Pyle's function in this regard. It begins with Pyle's insistently and repeatedly calling Fowler by
his Christian name, Thomas. This summons is in itself significant, for it stresses that Fowler is, as his first name can imply,
filled with righteous doubt. In the dream itself Fowler sees himself "walking down a long, empty road looking for a turning
which never came. The road unwound like a tape machine
with a uniformity that would never have altered if the voice
hadn't broken in—first of all like a voice crying in pain from a
tower and then suddenly a voice speaking to me personally"
(*QA,* p. 144). If Pyle is misguided, he still is not lost in one
sense, for he does have a faith in something outside himself.
Most important, though, Pyle's voice represents that of the
young calling out in need. Then the dream merges into half-
dream, and as it does it gravitates toward a more complete implication of what Pyle means to Fowler:

> Under my breath I said, "Go away, Pyle. Don't come
> near me. I don't want to be saved."
> "Thomas." He was hitting at my door, but I lay pos-
> sum as though I were back in the rice field and he was an
> enemy (*QA,* p. 144).

In a very real sense, Pyle is his enemy in love and in war. More symbolically, the American threatens his false peace. This dream, then, serves to indicate that, by continuously forcing himself on Fowler's conscience, Pyle awakens it.

As has already been suggested, what Fowler finally awakens to is not Pyle's personal ideas of conscience. Pyle's vision of life has a fanatical gleam. He has entered into the struggle of life with the weapons of innocence and devotion, but they are both tarnished by intellectual prejudice and they consequently serve to destroy him. He is dedicated to a political vision of life; but, as Fowler realizes, he has no real notion of "what the whole affair's about. . . . He never saw anything he hadn't heard in a lecture-hall, and his writers and his lecturers made a fool of him. When he saw a dead body he couldn't even see the wounds. A Red menace, a soldier of democracy" (*QA,* p. 27). Being only able to see in the abstract, he is blind to the essential truth which Fowler eventually understands: "Suffering is not increased by numbers: one body can contain all the suffering the world can feel" (*QA,* p. 204).

Because Pyle's innocence is not based on experience and creative imagination, it is sinister and lethal. Such innocence, which is really the worst kind of adult ignorance, is a terrible disease. It "always calls mutely for protection when we would be so much wiser to guard ourselves against it: innocence is like a dumb leper who has lost his bell, wandering the world, meaning no harm" (*QA,* p. 34). After the explosion in the square, the dangerous extent of Pyle's political chastity comes home to Fowler, and so he decides on a radical step of involvement. He decides to destroy his antagonist; however, he acts not from a motive of vengeance but with an imaginative sympathy. He has tried to make Pyle recognize that there is nothing gallant in atrocity by forcing his shoe into the blood of the victims of the terrorist violence the American has subsidized, but he can see that Pyle does not understand the significance of the act. Thus Fowler concludes: "What's the good? he'll always be innocent, you can't blame the innocent, they are always guiltless. All you can do is control them or eliminate them. Innocence is a kind of insanity" (*QA,* p. 182).

If Fowler were only interested in the economy of pain, he could find sufficient self-justification for conspiring in the death of Pyle. But his conscience haunts him because of a terrible dilemma, for although he fears and hates what Pyle stands for, he nevertheless is the only one who truly becomes interested in the character and the fate of the American. As he will come to understand more clearly through his subsequent relationship with Granger, a boisterous transmogrification of the quiet American, once one has entered the unexplored territory of another human being, he is mesmerized by the vision of human failure—that is, unless he has a lack of imagination. Having arrived at the point where he understands that he must destroy Pyle in order to save others and himself, he nevertheless has some compassion for his viction and he feels like a Judas who betrays someone who was his savior primarily in the sense that the latter needed him. This is why the final words of Fowler's confession have the quality of genuine torment and ambiguity: "everything had gone right with me since he had died, but how I wished there existed someone to whom I could say that I was sorry" (*QA*, p. 211).

In these words of repentance Fowler's renewed sense of guilt is conspicuous and is actually the clearest sign of his salvation. An important question, however, must still be asked: who is that "someone" of his supplication?

That the question should be necessary is plainly Greene's intent. He has often expressed his complex vision of life through "carefully nurtured ambiguity."[12] He has been, as Philip Stratford says, "irresistibly drawn to frontiers. Where they didn't exist, he invented them; where they did, he assiduously sought out some of the remoter of them; once across, he hearkened back to the place he had left; when caught in some no-man's land, he suffered from it, exquisitely."[13] Fowler is obviously a kind of extension of Greene. He, too, experiences the fine tension between exile and membership. And as he crosses into various regions of the mind, he suffers the agony of abandonment or alienation. At the end of his journey his anguish is particularly acute because he is entering the territory of faith.

It is perhaps possible that the "someone" of Fowler's last words is God. The critic Pryce-Jones, for one, declares that the reference *must* be to God, and his reasoning certainly has considerable merit. As the argument goes, Fowler's attempt to live in detachment is bound to fail because, when he finds himself in a dilemma which requires a moral decision, he feels at a loss due to the fact that he cannot draw on any religious resources. His neutrality is especially certain to fail in a situation of violence, for if he elects not to give spiritual value to life, then he must rate life even higher than the religious person does since he believes this life to be the only one. When Fowler is made to choose sides despite his skepticism, he goes beyond his subjective assumption and, supposing the existence of higher values, takes part in Pyle's death. What can these lofty ends be, asks Pryce-Jones, but those postulated by God?[14] The answer is that there might be other great ends which can be posited by other forms of faith.

The truth is that Fowler seems to be as set in his atheism at the end of the story as he is at the beginning. What is different in his outlook is that he is more inclined to express a reverence of life. In this regard, it should be pointed out that the critical view that *The Quiet American* is a novel about the absence of religion is imprecise.[15] On the contrary, it turns out to be just what Greene calls it, a "kind of morality about religion."[16] In this novel there is a far-ranging exploration of the differences and the affinities between the varieties of religious experience. In his Catholic novels, Greene was more categorical and restrictive on the subject of religion. In *The Quiet American* his "view of human comedy is more tolerant," as one critic puts it, and "his personal religious affiliation less apparent."[17] If in the earlier novels there exists on the part of Greene a tendency to mock religions other than Catholicism, now only the mongrel Caodaists are selected for a certain amount of irony because of their technicolor fabrications. As a whole, the tone of *The Quiet American* is more indulgent because Greene has apparently determined that the form of a faith is beside the point and that the only thing that counts is whether or not a faith is wed to a creative view of life. What saves Fowler, after all, is not a supernatural manifestation but the sight of the blood of Pyle's victims. Grace may or may not be participating in the fate of Fowler; God may or may not be listening to his confession. In the Catholic novels the devastating presence of God's grace is made quite explicit. But in *The Quiet American* Greene's implicit purpose is to suggest that there are perhaps other forms of salvation.

Critical Misconceptions

As has already been suggested, there remain critics who, due to the influence of the Catholic novels, find it difficult to shift with Greene to new grounds. The Catholic press in particular has had a painful time in adjusting to the drift of those novels which have followed *The End of the Affair*. The unfortunate result has been a certain amount of intellectual acrobatics which has led to some extraordinary, contorted interpretations.[18] What must be understood is that if Greene wrote his earlier novels in a spirit of Catholic commitment with the characters struggling in a demoniacal world, now he writes, in the words of Philip Stratford, as "a recruit to the Foreign Legion" of the church.[19] Beginning with *The Quiet American* he becomes especially concerned with the politics of deontology.

Following Greene's increasing drift into the political arena in his later novels, many critics have predictably begun to stress the existential qualities which can be discovered in his works. Because of his persistent concern with the paradoxes of compassion and because of his grasp of the ambiguity of goodness, not to mention his abhorrence of power politics, the French existentialists in particular have decided to adopt him as one of their own.[20] To be sure, Greene has always been a Sartrian existentialist of sorts, for he has consistently been attracted by the individuals having the courage of risking choice and engagement.[21] Not surprisingly, he has also been labelled a Christian existentialist.[22] As in the case of his Catholicism, however, Greene's beliefs are too unorthodox to be easily categorized. One should recognize that there is a certain existentialist disposition in Greene's novels, for that constitutes a dimension of his world. Yet it is rather futile to try to fit it into a pre-conceived niche, for Greene's form of existentialism is private and primarily aesthetic.

If the critical concern with the form of Greene's existentialism has failed to fit him neatly into a philosophical school or category, it has succeeded in a more important way. The swell of existentialist interpretations of Greene's works has made plain that he has always been searching for a means by which an individual would be allowed to live in dignity despite the apparently absurd pattern life may impose on one.

In this regard, it should be pointed out that one can discover a note of comic absurdity in *The Quiet American*. For example, there is Fowler trying to suppress a sneeze that would give his and Pyle's position away as enemy soldiers hunt in the night for survivors after blowing up the watchtower where the two had been. Or there is the farcical scene in which Fowler is forced to translate his rival's marriage proposal to Phuong. The laughter at the comedy of life is still muted. Absurdity will, however, develop as an increasingly obvious theme in the following books, until it becomes clear Greene is persuaded that, in his own words, beneath "the enormous shadow of the Cross it is better to be gay."[23]   The nature of this gayety may often be no more than the sad laughter at the comedy of the absurd pattern man's life might follow.   Still, in Greene's later eschatologies there is sufficient reason to be gay because the resurrection of the heart is an endless possibility if one is willing to take the risk of human involvement.

V.
COMIC DIRECTIONS

Three years after *The Quiet American,* Greene brought forth *Our Man In Havana* (1958), a book which was both typical and new for him. Like so many of his previous works, it refers to such large issues as personal responsibility, commitment, imagination, faith, and love. Moreover, it is cast in the framework of a thriller, and stylistic similarities between it and Greene's previous fiction abound. However, it represents something of a departure, too. This resides in its aggressively comic nature. Greene's previous work may often have had some comic elements or undertones. Now, however, comedy, or more precisely farce, comes to the fore not only as a method but also as a theme.

The situation which Greene sets up begins earnestly enough. Wormold, the protagonist of the story, is pictured as a dull, worried middle-aged man who sells vacuum cleaners to make a living and, rather desperately, tries to raise the daughter who was left him by an abandoning wife. Then he is unexpectedly engaged as an agent for the British Secret Service, and the story quickly develops into a hilariously sharp-edged burlesque which, if one didn't know better, might have been written by a writer such as Kingsley Amis. Once Wormold takes the job, which he does mainly for the extra money he needs to support his daughter's expensive desires, he reluctantly faces up to the fact that the Service requires intelligence reports from him. In a fit of desperation, or more properly inspiration, he begins to invent an organization of personal recruits and sends in reports which detail an ominous new military build-up in a remote area of Cuba, but which actually consists of sketches of the Atomic Pile vacuum cleaners he has been unsuccessfully trying to sell at his shop. For a time, things go amazingly well for Wormold. But eventually there are some unforseen, painful consequences; and in the end events simply catch up with his masquerade. Before that happens, though, Wormold manages to fall in love (with a beautiful agent sent to help him), to make provisions for the future of his daughter, and, most important, to discover a creative new way of life.

The framework of the story itself indicates that Wormold resembles those protagonists in Greene's previous novels who are rejuvenated by acts of imagination, responsibility, and love. However, the very last paragraph of the novel underlines the fact that Greene wants us to understand that Wormold's salvation depends even more on the factor of "madness." In those final lines, Wormold is made to express his fear that in the future "he would never be quite mad enough."[1] This is, obviously, a way of saying that this quality has become so essential to him he doesn't wish to imagine life without it.

Precisely what kind of "madness" is under consideration? In the context of this story, it refers on one level to risk taking. On another, more important, level it refers to those qualities inherent in the traditional kind of clown the story alludes to on more than one occasion. This clown, because of his permanent act of comedy, goes through life unchanged by the various political waves or the age's great catastrophes or discoveries. In other words, the clown endures because of his ageless and somewhat anarchic farcical behavior; and all this applies to Wormold's final disposition. Even if he may not yet fully realize it himself, Wormold has finally reached the point where he has acquired a permanent strength to face the pressures of the contemporary world because of the comic vision he has learned to adopt.

Although it seems clear that Wormold's final thoughts about "madness" represent the primary theme, this does not mean, unfortunately, that Greene treats it with complete success in this novel. The problem is that this and other serious aspects of the book appear at times to be superimposed rather than merged completely with the story. One of Greene's critics has speculated that this problem is the result of his trying too hard for "the impossible conjunction of comedy and farce."[2] This is perhaps close to the truth, but not quite. The real cause behind the occasionally divided nature of the novel seems to be that Greene had embarked on a theory which he hadn't yet fully developed in his mind, the theory of the close relationship between tragedy, farce, and absurdity. Due to this somewhat split, inchoate quality, *Our Man In Havana* can't be listed as one of Greene's major accomplishments. Still, it is in a way indispensable to a consideration of Greene's total work, because it does at least offer im-

portant transitional value. When it is considered in its chronological position between *The Quite American* and *A Burnt-Out
Case,* it becomes clear that this novel actually reflects the fact
that Greene was undergoing a significant development in his outlook. *Our Man In Havana* picks up on the factor of absurdity
adumbrated in *The Quite American,* develops the technique of its
comic possibilities, and then at least points to the idea which becomes prominent in Greene's thoughts thereafter—that the existential absurdity of life is allied to the positive, necessary values
of comedy and farce.

A Burnt-Out Case

On the surface, *A Burnt-Out Case* (1961) may not seem to
belong under the heading of comedy at all, since in some ways it
appears to be the grimmest of Greene's novels. There is, to begin
with, the setting, a leper colony where the victims rot from that
frightful disease and are not even safe from other plagues. Particularly shocking are the torments of the man with elephantiasis
who is forced to carry his enormous testicles in his hands and the
woman with palsied eyelids who can never close her eyes against
the unmerciful light. The central character is not a leper in the
physical sense, yet his suffering is, as we discover, even more profound, for he is a spiritual grotesque who has been plagued by
the demands of an enlarged sexual organ and a kind of blindness,
too. Nevertheless, joined much more successfully to the tragical
side than in *Our Man In Havana,* there also exists a broad sense of
farce in this book. Because the tragic aspect is so powerful, and
the farce as a result constricted by this tension, the story never
becomes "funny," of course. However, as Greene crosses and re-
crosses the boundaries of farce and tragedy, he finally leaves the
impression that life is neither extreme but is instead a dark
comedy.[3]
In the Catholic tetralogy we are made to be aware of God's
eye watching the human drama. In *A Burnt-Out Case* God may
be watching still, but it is the novelist's presence we are more
conscious of, melancholy, brooding, yet deeply ironic and
whimsical, too. This novel actually abounds with a sense of outrageous comedy. There is the Superior's confusion about the
function of a bidet; it looks like a footbath to him, and he would

like to have several for the leprosarium. There is the droll anec-
dote of a taciturn Greek who buys a car almost as ancient as he
in order to run down his cuckold as an expression of disapproval.
But most significant, there is the fact that the climax of the protagonist's story has the quality of farce. His life's tale turns on
the time-honored situation of an older husband wrongly accus-
ing a man with a notorious reputation of violating his young
wife. As the victim of the accusation himself says, his story
seems to have become a comedy which could be entitled "The
innocent adulterer."[4] Needless to say, in a pure farce the blame-
less adulterer would not be shot down.

The way in which Querry dies seems to be a meaningless
absurdity, but only if his last minutes are isolated from previous
developments. If put in perspective, the shots which kill him
actually trigger an epiphany which comes at the end of a long
journey into the darkness of self-discovery. That he dies being
able to laugh at himself is, as we are led to recognize, the sign
that he has finally found himself.

Querry's name obviously suggests to us that he is enigmatic
and on an elusive quest. It also implies he is the quarry of a past
that pursues him and a conscience that haunts him. He is a
frightened passenger of time, for his memory tells him that at its
core there is a terrible vacancy. Typical of Greene's method, we
can begin only gradually to fill in the specific reasons for his
fear; but at the very start of his physical journey we see him in a
setting which serves as a metaphor both for his life and, since his
life attains a parabolic function, for modern life in general:

> His journey began in the great all-but-empty airport built
> for a world-exhibition which had closed a long time ago.
> One could walk a mile through the corridor without see-
> ing more than a scattering of human beings. In an im-
> mense hall people sat apart. . . . They looked like statues
> in an art gallery (*B-OC,* p. 172).

The desolation, the splendid waste, and the enormous vacancy
described here correspond to Querry's condition as he embarks
for a different realm.

When we see Querry at the beginning of the novel, he is
merely searching for escape. He is nameless, referred to simply
as the cabin-passenger, for it is anonymity that he yearns for. A
curiosity of his own condition is one clear sign of intellectual

animation. It takes the form of a quaint, self-deprecatory entry in his journal, however, which implies a deep exhaustion: "I feel discomfort, therefore I am alive" (*B-OC*, p. 1). This Cartesian parody indicates to us that, just as his boat has entered the zone of sleeping sickness, so has his heart. At the beginning of his journey Querry could have described his condition in the words of the novel's Danteian epigraph: "I did not die, yet nothing of life remained." Yet the evidence that Querry has an understanding of where he has been and retains some curiosity of where he is are signs he is also approaching the region of renewal.

The geographical territory he is entering is the Congo, which to Greene has always been an important region of the mind, too. In the dedicatory letter of the novel Greene explains that he elected the Congo as the setting because its isolation from international politics and daily affairs allowed him a better opportunity to give dramatic expression to his chosen subject. Beyond his belief in the aesthetic advantage of secluding his characters, Greene's motive for choosing the Congo must have been based on the personal experience of the revitalizing journey to Africa he had earlier described in *Journey Without Maps*. Relative to this point is the fact that Greene's personal experiences are frequently, and as a rule quite subconsciously, transmuted into the eventual make-up of major characters. Thus it's no exaggeration to claim that when Greeene explains the lure of Africa in *Journey Without Maps*, he is anticipating the story of Querry to a large extent. One need only summarize Greene's main points of reasoning which give thematic shape to the travel book to discover that this is so.[5]

As Greene recalled, living in a brutal age, he experienced a yearning for what he perceived to be the inscrutable darkness of the African continent shaped, as if by design, as a heart where life seems fresher and men appear to live in the juvenescence of time. This dark land does not represent an edenic alternative to the decadence of Europe, since the devil is an ever-present reality to its people. It is precisely because the devil is so real to the Africans, however, that he thinks they may not be as lost as the sophisticates of the older civilizations. Being able to experience supernatural terror because of their creative imaginations, being able to surrender to the mysteries surrounding them, they have a less jaundiced view of life and are able to live more spontaneously and intensely. That is, they look on life as Greene remembers he did as a child.

Greene stated his motive for going to Africa as "a curiosity to discover if one can from what we have come, to recall at which point we went astray."[6] As he expected, what he found there "reinforced a sense of disappointment with what man had made out of the primitive, what he had made out of childhood."[7] But if he was disappointed in this way, in another he was not, because there he discovered the rejuvenating power of myth and ritual.[8] Moreover, as has previously been emphasized, he surprised himself with the discovery that he had a strong desire to go on living. What happened to Greene in Africa describes in large part what happens to Querry. Of course, Querry's original motives for going there are not *consciously* the same as were those of Greene, for he has no intention of going on a voyage of self-exploration; and if he chooses Africa, it is because he feels that it is simply the last place on earth.

When Querry stops at the leprosarium, he finds himself in a physical hell where he has illusions of safety from his past, but he cannot escape his egoistical hell without a mental journey, too. He arrives in a conditoin of emotional lethargy and spiritual decay because his interest in anything outside his physical comfort has atrophied. He has been maimed by his progressive loss of faith in his vocation, in human love, and in God. He confronts the horror of his aridity with a kind of dignified stoicism, but underneath the surface impassiveness there lies a moldering self-pity. Because he can take only himself seriously, he feels taunted by the laughter of others. When he stops at a seminary for a night on the way to the leper colony and observes the playfulness of the priests and natives, he feels "abandoned . . . to his own region where laughter was like the unknown syllables of an enemy tongue" (*B-OC*, p. 9). However, because Querry has been probing his malady and continues to do so even as he approaches the painful truth about himself, a close anlaysis will show that he is actually already entering the period of recovery.

At the end of the first chapter of the novel Querry makes a revealing observation: "I suffer from nothing. I no longer know what suffering is. I have come to an end of all that too" (*B-OC*, p. 10). If he is to experience a renewal, he must learn to distinguish between mere discomfort and the pain of living. In the world of Greene's novels the condition of suffering must precede regeneration. Only a child can be free of the burden of pain, since he has not yet entered the area of failure. Once a

person has gone beyond adolescence, only a boundless ego allows
him to commit himself to his own success. If he lives in a state
of self-worship, he does not feel the pain of others and as a
result loses the religious sense of life which is a characteristic of
childhood.   Failing to accept the burden of suffering that is
common to the human condition, he becomes a spiritual leper,
for the alternative to pain is mutilation.

It is through his relationship with his leper servant, Deo
Gratias, that Querry experiences certain feelings which first tell
us his anesthesia is wearing down. At the beginning he is hardly
aware of the existence of Deo Gratias. When one day the servant
does not appear to do his work, however, Querry responds with
feelings which reveal some clear interest in another human being.
When he hears that Deo Gratias had been seen going into the
bush, he goes in search of him as the night approaches because,
he tells himself, he is merely driven by a "vestige of intellectual
curiosity" (*B-OC,* p. 59). He cannot yet realize there might be
more to his action since he "had lived with inertia so long that
he examined his 'interest' with clinical detachment" (*B-OC,*
p. 59). But after he finds his servant in a gap into which he had
accidentally fallen and out of which the leper could not make his
way, Querry stays the night with him and comforts him against
his crippling fear. This night becomes a crisis of involvement for
Querry, and after it his feelings for others begin to return. As he
later examines the significance of this night, he recognizes that
it was "a night when things begin," when for the first time he
could remember he had "an odd feeling" that he was needed
(*B-OC,* p. 61).

During this night Deo Gratias expresses his yearning for a
mysterious place called Pendéle. He had set out to go there
when he met with his accident, for he felt an overpowering urge
to return to this palce which he had seen as a child and which
induces the recollection of joy and devotion. Querry will later
ask Deo Gratias to take him along the next time his servant feels
possessed by the desire to go there, even though he realizes that
it has actually become just an imagined region to the leper.
Because Pendéle has come to represent a return to innocence
and hope for Querry, it is his wish to go there which is conse-
quential.   His expressed desire is a measure of his liberating
imagination.

As his vanity shrinks, Querry no longer excludes others
from his concern and begins to recognize his own reflection in

other persons. His most conspicuous alter-ego is Deo Gratias. But this does not mean his self-analysis can stop with the examination of his servant. For one thing, there is an important distinction between the two. When Querry finds Deo Gratias in the gap of earth, the leper's "knuckles felt as a rock might that has been eroded for years by the weather" and he was "warm and wet like a hummock of soil . . ." (*B-OC,* pp. 60-61). This description tells us that Deo Gratias is the natural man whose existence has the strength of simplicity. He howls with panic the night Querry keeps the vigil with him because fear is an elemental, necessary reality to him. On the other hand, the peace he identifies with his memory of Pendéle is also a firm possibility to him. Querry, though, is a creature of sophistication, and hence his fears and hopes are more abstract and the process of his rehabilitation more tortuous.

The mutilation of Querry has gone much deeper than has that of Deo Gratias. The servant has lost his fingers and toes, and so he is forced to do the simplest tasks with great difficulty. In a different way, Querry has lost more, and he is reminded in part of his form of mutilation by the ironic example of Rycker. Rycher, whose palm-oil factory is an appropriate indicator of his unctuousness, pursues Querry because he wishes to identify himself with the image of martyrdom he has chosen for the famous architect. He talks eagerly about his lost vocation as a priest, of his failing relationship with his wife, and of his love for God; but his words have the hollow sound of self-admiration. It is not surprising that Querry has an almost immediate feeling of revulsion for Rycker; but as he begins to reconstruct his past, Querry comes to the realization that Rycker is an amplified image of what he has been. Late in the story Querry can face this unpleasant fact because, as he tells Rycker, he is no longer willing to play his past role:

> I begin to think we are not so different, you and I. We don't know what love is. You pretend to love a god because you love no one else. But I won't pretend. All I have left me is a certain regard for truth. It was the best sides of the small talent I had. You are inventing all the time. . . . You've even invented this idea of me to justify yourself. But I won't play your game, Rycker (*B-OC,* p. 169).

Not surprisingly, Rycker twists the words of Querry, because he does not have the imagination to picture anyone else in any way different from his preconceived view. Consequently, he will continue to torment Querry, romanticizing him as a saint until he suspects him of impregnating his wife, Marie, at which point Rycker suddenly looks on Querry as a Judas figure who has betrayed his high aspirations. The false piety of Rycker excites a strong disgust in Querry, as a result of which he experiences a certain re-awakening of spiritual longing.

If Querry can see the false religion of his past when he looks at Rycker, he can recognize the devouring cynicism remaining within him when he looks at Parkinson. Querry is naturally frightened of Parkinson when he materializes like an evil spirit to shatter the illusion of peace he clings to.[9] As he later tells Parkinson, "You are my looking-glass. I can talk to a looking-glass, but one can be a little afraid of one too. It returns such a straight image" (*B-OC*, p. 133). Peace, however, is not possible in the world of Greene without the prior torments of self-examination. Querry must face himself as he is reflected in the person of Parkinson in particular if he is to be delivered from the spectre of betraying his vocation.

Parkinson is a journalist who has arrived to gather information about the famous architect rumored to have withdrawn from the world to a leper colony. His intention, though, is not to write the truth so much as it is to feed his reader's appetite for sensationalism. Truth does not count for him anymore because he is a kind of spoilt priest. He has long ago betrayed his profession, and now he exudes the strong scent of decay. There is a strange attraction about him just as there was about the Yusef character in *The Heart of the Matter;* but more easily than his counterpart Querry can recognize the source of this allurement for what it is. Parkinson is both fat with the sloth of his existence and hollow from the decadence of his life. He is another spiritual leper who carries his mutilation "on the surface of his skin like phosphorus, impossible to mistake. Virtue had died long ago within that mountain of flesh for lack of air. A priest might not be shocked by human failings, but he could be hurt or disappointed; Parkinson would welcome any kind of failing. Nothing would hurt Parkinson or disappoint him but the size of a cheque" (*B-OC*, p. 124).

It is possible that Parkinson is affected more deeply than anyone realizes by the example of Querry. In a statement which

might serve as the theme of his disappointed life, he says late in
the book: "A man's got to believe a bit or contract out altogether" (*B-OC*, p. 198). Whether Parkinson indeed is finally
healed from his cynicism is not certain; it is clear, though, that
his doubts have had the catalytic function of arousing in Querry
a new awareness. It is in Parkinson's presence that he can speculate about the nature of love. Surprisingly for a man who has
been cynical about all emotion, Querry makes a connection between human and divine love; he now concludes that "you can't
believe in a god without loving a human being or love a human
being without believing in god" (*B-OC*, p. 130). And shortly
after this revelation Querry is able to make his first declaration of
repentance for the injury he has caused through false love and
he can be moved by the wish that he cause no more pain:

> I shall do no more harm, he thought, with the kind of
> happiness a leper must feel when he is freed at last by his
> seclusion from the fear of passing on contagion to another
> (*B-OC*, p. 135).

As we have seen, in Greene's world one cannot be at peace
in isolation. Only through involvement with the fates of others
can one hope to break through the sphere of guilt. Yet in crossing over to human commitment, one finds himself in a turbulent
region where there is present a constant danger of relationships
swirling out of control. Querry has been in this region before,
but only as an outsider who measured his passion with precision.
Now that he is about to re-enter it, he is less rigid. No longer
does he depend on sexual prowess as a measure of love. Having
gone through a process of self-examination, he has found within
himself a reservoir of innocence. Still, if he is now less guilty of
violating others for the sake of his own pleasure, he is also more
innocent of the calculating ways of the heart.

Therefore, when late in the book Querry inadvertently finds
himself getting involved in the unfortunate fate of Marie, he
thinks wrongly: "poor frightened beast—this one was too young
to be a great danger. It was only when they were fully grown
you couldn't trust them with your pity" (*B-OC*, p. 174). His
new lack of guile is a measure of his rehabilitation; yet the painful paradox is that he is now also more vulnerable, because with
increased compassion he is more prone to be deluded by the
various corrupt forms of sentiment. He is certainly wrong in his

estimation of Marie, and the ultimate consequence is that he pays for his illusion with his life.

The reason why Querry is beguiled by Marie in the first place is the same one which has drawn him to Deo Gratias, Rycker, and Parkinson—the memory of what he has been and the realization of what he is becoming. He is strongly reminded by her of his past with another woman by the name of Marie. The former Marie, too, was trapped in a relationship where she was forced to make love with a mechanical partner. The fact that the desperation of the former Marie reached the point where she committed suicide is the most disturbing memory of Querry, and it is the primary factor in obliging him to become engaged in the problems of the present Marie. As was true of Scobie, the fear of being in any way responsible for a possible suicide has paradoxical consequences for Querry, because while it leads to a certain paralysis of will, it also becomes a gauge of his humanity.

Querry finally reaches the point where he can admit that his enormous ego was responsible for the death of his Marie. He faces the unpleasant fact that if, before she killed herself, he had managed to get her back on several occasions, it was just to satisfy his vanity which would be hurt if he were left by a woman. If anyone was going to do the leaving, it was going to be he. Thus when Rycker's wife falsely claims him as the father of the child she is carrying, he realizes that "he was confronted by an egoism as absolute as his own" (*B-OC*, p. 219). He once thought this Marie was a mere child trapped by inexperience; now he has grown to recognize her kind of innocence to be highly dangerous because it was based on selfish ignorance. Yet despite the fact that he finally learns to recognize her for what she is, he does not take any decisive action against her lies. He attempts to deny the accusation he has been her lover, of course, but because he has a full understanding of her desperation, he is trapped by compassion.

Querry started his voyage into the Congo by noting that he was able to feel merely physical discomfort. Now as he considers the panic of Rycker's wife, he finds that he has reached a point of renewal. As he tells Colin, the doctor at the leprosarium, he has become capable of experiencing disembodied pain. Querry can now agree with the doctor that suffering is important because it serves to join one to the condition of humanity. Because Querry has arrived at where he can say "I suffer, therefore I am," Colin declares him as cured (*B-OC,* p. 221).

This announcement of Querry's cure can be trusted both because of the novel's strategies already revealed and because of the doctor's unique and complex function in the story. In very real terms, Colin is a scientist who has a deep understanding of the human condition of suffering. He makes a career of diagnosing and healing the torments of lepers. He is also a specialist in psychic mutilation. As a result, he can recognize the malady of Querry for what it is and can trace the steps of his gradual recovery. At the same time, he acts as still another alter-ego to Querry, and an especially faithful yet ironic one, for he still retains what Querry has lost, a vocation and a guiding faith. Moreover, the doctor assumes the choric role that priests tend to have in Greene's Catholic novels by commenting on the significance of the action and by restoring a sense of perspective to the world of the leprosarium at the end of the story.[10]

It is Colin's diagnosis of the original reason for Querry's coming to the colony which startles the patient into expressing the sad truth about himself for the first time. When Colin suggests that Querry has come to die, the patient's rejoinder becomes a kind of self-palpation: "That *was* in my mind. But chiefly I wanted to be in an empty place, where no new building or woman would remind me that there was a time when I was alive, with a vocation and a capacity to love—if it was love. The palsied suffer, their nerves feel, but I am one of the mutilated, doctor" (*B-OC,* p. 47). Now knowing the form of his illness, the first step in recovery, Querry asks Colin if he can be cured. The doctor's answer explains why Querry's convalescence is at first necessarily so dysphoric: "Perhaps your mutilations haven't gone far enough yet. When a man comes here too late the disease has to burn itself out" (*B-OC,* p. 47).

After Colin's diagnosis, Querry can be seen constantly examining himself, fingering his sore spots, testing against new mutilations, analyzing the extent of his malady. Similar to what Colin does with his leper patients, Querry keeps a chronicle of his progress. One day he records the following in his journal: "I haven't enough feeling left for human beings to do anything for them out of pity" (*B-OC,* p. 52). Because his anesthesia is so persistent, that same day he writes a revealing note to the doctor which is an attempt to explain himself but which also turns into a cry of desolation. He tries to insist to Colin that there is a gulf between them he can never cross. "What I have built, I have always built for myself, not for the glory of God or the pleasure of a purchaser," he writes. "Don't talk to me of human beings. Human beings are not my country" (*B-OC*, p. 53). But the half-sentence which ends the note, described as being "like a plan, from a ship's deck off which a victim has been thrust," tells us Querry both fears and desires to enter the region of Colin. He is willing, he writes, to do anything "in reason" for the doctor; but when he adds "don't ask me to try to revise. . . ," he indicates his realization this is really Colin's silent prescription and that it is the only means of escaping his sphere of exclusion.

The fact that not long thereafter Querry does have a tentative experience of personal revision despite his anxiety is made apparent when he attempts to make his first joke. Colin has been telling Querry about his observation that the old lepers retain a deep sense of hope. Since the patients he is talking about are all dying, he says that "their last disease is hope" (*B-OC*, p. 63). Querry's subsequent comment, made with his face "twisted into the rictus of a laugh," is that if he should turn up missing, the doctor would know to look for him in the region of hope. Querry has now arrived at the point where he has the capacity to yearn for liberation from and yet at the same time to smile at his own baroque drama.

At this point it becomes clear that Querry's malady has run its course, for laughter is a major symbol of recovery in this book.[11] Subsequently, Querry surprises himself with a declaration to Colin that he had found happiness at the colony. Colin soon becomes certain that Querry is indeed a burnt-out case, because he notes the patient's negative reaction when he spends the night with Deo Gratias and a second such reaction when Querry reveals some interest in the pain of life after observing an especially pitiable case the doctor is treating. Querry has learned that, as Colin says, "the search for suffering and the remembrance of suffering are the only means we have to put ourselves in touch with the whole human condition. With suffering we become part of the Christian myth" (*B-OC*, p. 141).

Many of Greene's Catholic readers were disturbed by the fact that in Colin he had created a totally admirable character who happens to be a declared atheist.[12] Without dwelling on this not unexpected development, it should be emphasized that if the doctor doesn't believe in God, he is nevertheless a man of faith. He believes that there is reason for hope because, as he sees it, life is a process of evolution, and even love is part of that process. He finds comfort in the possibility that love could evolve as dramatically in man as has his grasp of technical matters. In fact, he thinks that in isolated cases such evolution may have already occurred. Christ and the saints, for example, come to his mind.[13] To Querry's remark that all this sounds as superstitious as the faith of the priests, Colin has the following rejoinder: "It's the superstition I live by" (*B-OC*, p. 144). He knows that one's faith may prove to be fallacious. Still, one has to gamble on it, for with a guiding belief, particularly if it is concerned with people, the form of one's life is neither empty nor absurd. Because Querry ultimately learns the truth of this view, the doctor is correct in pronouncing him as having been cured "of all but his success" after he has been shot by Rycker (*B-OC*, p. 234). Although Querry's form of death certainly carries some elements of irony, it is not unavailingly absurd because it comes after the successful end of a spiral journey of self-exploration. Querry, by getting involved with the work of the leoprosarium and with certain people about him, has discovered that at the heart of the human state there exists a region of innocence and that, by going ever deeper into himself, he can find a purer, more generous self.

As has been pointed out, Querry's success in finding himself depends in large part on the recognition of his image in various other persons. What should be added is that, just as in the case of Fowler, he is constrained to go through a series of confessions because that is the most certain means of self-recognition and redemptive humility. While Querry reveals more and more of the truth about himself to his listeners, he feels the poison of pride draining out of him and experiences the strange sensation of peace settling in. He has several such purgative confessional dialogues, notably with Parkinson and Colin. But the one occasion during which he confesses most fully occurs when he tries to soothe and divert Rycker's wife with a story the night before she is to find out whether or not she is pregnant. He warns Marie that she is not to confuse the jeweller of the narrative with the story teller; however, the similarity between the two is all too obvious.[14] It is the story of a gifted artist who, his ego growing boundless because he was never made to experience failure or suffering, discovered that he had lost his ability to love, to believe, and to create. As Querry continues the tale, he experiences an elated "sense of freedom and release, like that of a prisoner who at last 'comes clean,' admitting everything to his inquistitor" (*B-OC*, p. 183). At the end of the story, as if at the end of a life, he has a vision of renewal.

For such a dark book all this might seem suspiciously like a happy ending. From a farcical standpoint, one can agree with the Superior that as far as Rycker, Marie, and Parkinson are concerned, their stories end with "quite a happy ending" since they "will have got what they wanted" though perhaps not what they at first expected (*B-OC*, p. 235). As for Querry, he found more than he expected when he started on his voyage since, as Colin declares, he had "learned to serve other people . . . and to laugh" (*B-OC*, p. 236). Moreover, he had found a faith to live by. Because Querry remains an essentially ambiguous man, we cannot be sure what form that faith ultimately took. The Superior would like to believe Querry had started looking for God and that, as Pascal thought, he had consequently already found Him before his death. But in the context of this book it is not at all necessary to conclude that Querry's faith had taken this direction. His last words—"this is absurd or else—" (*B-OC*, p. 233)— leave more than one possibility open. Pryce-Jones can offer the plausible argument that what crosses Querry's mind before he can finish the statement is that God must be either working through and for him, so that even his sensual and spiritual exhaustion are "just the catalysts of his salvation," or God is not, in which case everything is simply absurd.[15] On the other hand, more than one critic has picked up the Kierkegaardian echo in these last words as a sign that the alternative to absurdity is an existential creed.[16] In the final analysis, though, Professor Gwen Boardman is correct in reminding us that Greene's declared purpose as a writer is not simply to offer answers to problems so much as to provide "the correct setting of a question."[17]

If the final form of Querry's belief is ambiguous, it's Greene's intention. What he wished to do in *A Burnt-Out Case*, he has said, was "to show various grades of belief and disbelief. . . . There was a fanatical believer in the novel; a good believer, the Superior of the mission, who was too busy to concern himself with doubt; and the doctor, who had a real belief in his atheism."[18] As for Querry, Greene said, his "faith was lost temporarily and came back."[19] It is revealing that Greene is careful not to name the specific cast of that faith, for this is not the most important thing. What matters is whether or not a faith is animated with compassion. In the end, all creative faiths are related. As we see in the novel, even those of the Catholic Superior and of the humanist doctor, so antithetical in some respects, are joined by a commitment to the consecration of life. Therefore, Querry's elliptical statement can be completed in more than one way, and this is a clear sign that, while grace was the necessary form of salvation in his Catholic novels, here Greene can imagine other means.[20]

After Greene finished writing *A Burnt-Out Case,* he made another of those provocative statements which have tended to entangle his critics in hasty judgments:

> As one grows older the writing of a novel does not become more easy, and it seemed to me when I wrote the last words that I had reached an age when another full-length novel was probably beyond my powers.[21]

Evidently because of the influence of this declaration of exhaustion, there followed some premature obituaries announcing the contraction of his powers and, as a corollary, the end of his creative dream. However, in his next novel, *The Comedians,* Greene revealed instead that his art was still vital and that his vision was, in fact, still expanding. In *Our Man In Havana* and *A Burnt-Out Case* he had been comparatively indefinite and tentative in his outlook. Now in *The Comedians,* and even more obviously in *Travels With My Aunt,* the novels which followed it, he took on the extravagant comedy of man with more boldness and clearer conviction.

The Comedians

Next to *Brighton Rock, The Comedians* (1966) seems to be Greene's most widely misunderstood novel.[22] The title fairly begs for the story to be understood along the lines of comedy. Nevertheless, many reviewers and critics ignored this fact and focused instead on its political side. Probably this was inevitable, since the story could be, and therefore was, read as a kind of exposé of Haiti as an example of a contemporary system of tyranny. Greene had done this sort of thing before, notably in *The Power and the Glory.* There he employed the setting of a politically corrupt land to throw the human and religious drama into relief. In *The Comedians* this is obviously his intent, also. This time, however, he is more explicit and subjectively intense in his depiction of the political backdrop than ever before, and this led to two consequences. One had to do with the organic unity of the book. If there is a significant flaw in the novel, it has to do with the fact that the background is sometimes depicted with such barely contained anger and brutal observation that the story of the characters and the fundamental theme are momentarily overwhelmed. The other had to do with the fact that the publication of the novel was for a time a political event. This might have been all to the good if it hadn't encouraged the kind of misreading of the book which has been alluded to. This notoriety was sparked by the fact that the dictator of Haiti, Papa Doc Duvalier, became so incensed by the book that he attempted to discredit it and the writer by means of official propaganda and published invective. Predictably enough, his efforts backfired, and the novel was instead praised by many readers as the kind of aggressive political novel which makes a difference in the world. Now that Papa Doc is long since dead, and it's easier to put the novel in a proper perspective, it's clear that the major intent in *The Comedians* was actually a culmination of the comic theme at work in *Our Man In Havana* and *A Burnt-Out Case.*

In *The Comedians* Greene goes further than he did in the previous two novels to explore what he imagined as the peculiar carnival of the modern age. What he sees at the end is that today's world has all the trappings of a farcical entertainment, though with serious punch-lines. To put it in metaphorical terms (and this is a novel which seems to demand such a perspective), one might say that Greene has envisioned the truth of something like the following. In our age, there are everywhere the games of chance, the side-shows, the corridors of horror, all apparently rigged by a practical joker of comical genius (*perhaps* God). As the participant is drawn along, he discovers that farce can quickly change to calamity, that a harlequin can transform into a fearful demon. If life is a comedy, it's a black comedy. Those who share in it and are sensitive to the real drama are driven to the extreme laughter of tears. In any event, like it or not, one is borne on a carousel which whirls on, spinning past the grotesques, the swindlers, and the various apparitions haunting the contemporary scene. Yet although the horror of life is real, so is the possibility of salvation. And this essential point is illustrated by the human drama Greene has chosen to set in Haiti, where a political monstrosity has, on one hand, darkened the wretched land but, on the other, inspired the light of self-sacrifice which may be found within men even under the most extreme or absurdly surprising conditions.[23]

Brown, the narrator and focal character of *The Comedians*, initially represents the hollow man whose life is empty of values. If he is committed to anything, it's merely to his survival in a turbulent world. Action, he knows, is dangerous, and involvement with people is certain to proliferate out of control. Only the man who adjusts himself to the violent rhythms of contemporary political ways is likely to survive. He is satisfied to merely watch while other passengers of the times strain with terrific effort to reach their various goals. Conversely, he is sure that no one has the strength to endure the ordeal to a meaningful conclusion. Therefore, when we see him at the first of the novel aboard a ship on the way to Haiti, he is returning to that land after a few months' absence not because of any feelings of allegiance but because the tide of events and fortune just happens to be flowing in this direction for him.

Brown is an outsider who at this point does not feel a part of the violence and terror gripping the wretched little country. He is going back because the hotel he has tried to sell in New York without success is there and because the mistress he has tried to forget is perhaps still waiting for him. Since he is rootless, he drifts in the direction of least resistance. As he washes upon the shore of Haiti, he finds that the dictatorship of Papa Doc is, if anything, more terrifying now than it was when he last saw it. Because he is merely a spectator of the drama, the agony of Haiti has no claims on his conscience at this time.

During the course of the next few months, however, Brown is forced by a series of events to enter into the violent action which has been revolving around him. As these events close in, Brown experiences a kind of moral vertigo which allows him to realize he has been a piece of human wreckage. At the end of the story we see that he is once more washed ashore, this time the Dominican Republic. But now there is a difference in him. Greene writes that Brown "is a person who could not be better than he is, although he would like to."[24] Yet as Greene has so often suggested, it is the wish in a man to be other than he is that's of ultimate importance. It is an indication that his conscience is animated with the anxiety of guilt, the one quality which distinguished the ethical man from the barbarian. So far as Greene is concerned, thought much more than action defines the man, and the need for hope instead of success best reveals his destiny.

As Brown recounts his story, it becomes a confession of failure. In the process of piecing his past experiences and the meaning of the present together, Brown begins to realize he has been incapable of love and faith without even being fully aware of it. This is true mainly because he has looked upon life as a meaningless farrago. The significant understanding he eventually arrives at is that *he* has been the clown. Because the clown is the center of the stylized comedy of the absurd, he is also its greatest victim. In the moments of clarity that such a clown inevitably experiences, he comes to the realization that the laughter is at his expense and his act is essentially tragic. Because the act of the clown is ageless, it might appear that Brown is indeed trapped in his role.[25] In the end, however, Brown is the intelligent comedian who is weeping within while he performs his antic ritual. Laughter mingled with tears is the dominant mood of the narrator, and in the course of his story it becomes clear this is the disposition necessary for a deliverance from despair.[26]

In his youth Brown was prepared for quite a different role, that of a priest. Although he tries to laugh it off, a remark by his mistress, Martha, suggesting he is perhaps a *prêtre manqué*, brings back certain longings which cause him to suffer intensely. He tries to assure himself his sexual prowess has taken the place of theology; yet as he makes love to Martha, he flings himself "into pleasure like a suicide on to a pavement."[27] In this moment of desperate self-disgust, Brown knows that the faith he was trained in by the Jesuits in Monte Carlo had the necessary quality of moral substance; but while "other boys fought with the demon of masturbation," he recalls, he "fought with faith" (*C*, p. 52). Then one afternoon, being a natural born actor, he bluffed his way into the Casino, where he quickly won at the gambling wheel and just as quickly experienced his first success in the game of love. When he finds himself in the bedroom of the seasoned woman whom he "won" in the Casino, however, something happens which will haunt him for the remainder of his life:

An odd thing happened as we lay on the bed. She was

finding me shy, frightened, difficult. Her fingers had no success, even her lips had failed their office, when into the room suddenly, from the port below the hill, flew a seagull. For a moment the room seemed spanned by the length of the white wings. She gave an exclamation of dismay and retreated: it was she who was scared now. I put out a hand to reassure her. The bird came to rest on a chest below a gold-framed looking-glass and stood there regarding us on its long stiltlike legs. It seemed as completely at home in the room as a cat and at any moment I expected it to begin to clean its plumage. My new friend trembled a little with fear, and suddenly I found myself as firm as a man and I took her with such ease and confidence it was as though we had been lovers for a long time. Neither of us during those minutes saw the seagull go, although I shall always think that I felt the current of its wings on my back as the bird sailed out again towards the port and the bay (*C,* p. 55).

This is a moment of magic for Brown, as near to a sacred epiphany as he comes. It is as fleeting as the seagull itself, but Brown will be pursued by its memory from then on. Only near the end of his peripatetic wanderings does he arrive at the realization that the enthralling peace he is searching for depends not on the complete surrender of another woman to his strength but on his own surrender to the urgent weakness of someone else.

Many years after the day when he lost not only his virginity but a certain visionary innocence as well, Brown arrives in Haiti to a note from his long-lost mother. He knows very little about her since she deserted him while he was a child, yet he feels sure she is an expert in the artificial gestures of love and little else. She has played her role well, he thinks, but as her comedy is about to end, there is little she can leave behind for her son except the memory of an entertaining performance and a hotel she has inherited. However, Brown eventually arrives at the realization that she has left him much more than this—the example of a vital love for life.[2 8]

The night of his mother's death Brown has a dream which indicates just how desperate his sense of dislocation is:

I was walking by the side of a lake in the moonlight and I was dressed like an altar-boy—I felt the magnetism of the

> still quiet water, so that every step I took was nearer to
> the verge, until the uppers of my black boots were sub-
> merged. Then a wind blew and the surge rose over the
> lake, like a small tidal wave, but instead of coming to-
> wards me, it went in the opposite direction, raising the
> water in a long retreat, so that I found I walked on dry
> pebbles and that the lake existed only as a gleam on the
> far horizon of the desert of small stones, which wounded
> me through a hole in my boots (*C*, p. 66).

Brown had lost his religious faith, and in the modern desert of
cynicism he has found nothing to replace it. What he does not
yet realize is that there are various forms of belief in the world
which can reanimate a person's sense of hope, and that one of
these is his mother's commitment to the sensual grace of life.
Because she has the imagination to retain such a vision of beauty
despite the political horror of her time, she is truly, as Dr. Magiot
says, "a great woman" (*C*, p. 68).

Later Brown takes to sleeping in his mother's room where
she had died and Marcel, her young lover, had committed suicide. The room is haunted by death, but death which was not
meaningless. Brown's mother had died during the moment of her
final sexual extravagance with her lover, and hence she wore "an
ambiguous smile of secret or even sensual satisfaction" instead
of the gaze of a corpse (*C*, p. 67). Marcel had hanged himself
in the misery of his longing for her. To Brown there might
have been something farcical about the whole episode at first.
Eventually, he finds himself looking at it from a different point
of view. When he cut Marcel down from his noose, he had found
a letter from his mother in the lover's pocket in which she admitted she was old and a bit of an actress but in which she also
asked Marcel to keep on pretending otherwise. "As long as we
pretend," she had written, "we escape. Pretend that I would die
for you and that you would die for me" (*C*, p. 242). In fact,
she does literally die of a heart seizure for Marcel. Therefore,
when Brown re-reads her letter sometime after his return from
the New York trip, he finds that instead of sounding absurd, the
message is "movingly phrased." Concerning Marcel, he concludes
"he had died for her, so perhaps he was no *comédien* after all.
Death is a proof of sincerity" (*C*, p. 242).

Although Brown's mistress does not die for him, she proves
she is not merely a false performer in another way. During a

party at which her husband calls upon all to be comedians together, she says:

> I'm no comedian. . . . My child vomited just now. You
> can smell it still on my hands. He was crying with pain.
> You talk about acting parts. I'm not acting any part. I
> do something. I fetch a basin. I fetch aspirin. I wipe his
> mouth. I take him into my bed (*C*, p. 125).

She will later admit to Brown that she might have been exag-
gerating her ordeal, but that was because she was irritated by the
talk which "made every one of us seem cheap and useless and
self-pitying. Perhaps we are, but we needn't revel in it. At
least I do things, don't I, even if they are bad things. I didn't
pretend not to want you. I didn't pretend I loved you that first
evening" (*C*, p. 126). When Brown asks her if she loves him now,
her answer is that she loves her son Angel. She may fail in her
marriage, but not in her child-like honesty and her devotion to
her son. If she has betrayed her marriage vow, it is the result of
a form of desperation which Brown recognizes as being akin to
truth.

A number of months later, after the affair between them
has ended, Brown finally learns to appreciate her directness to a
full extent and to realize that she was indeed no mere comedian:

> She played no part. She answered exactly what I asked.
> She never claimed to like a thing that she disliked or to
> love something to which she was indifferent. If I had
> failed to understand her, it was because I failed to ask her
> the right questions, that was all. It was true that she was
> no comedian. She had kept the virtue of innocence, and
> I know now why I loved her. In the end the only quality
> but beauty which attracts me in a woman is that
> vague thing, "goodness." The woman in Monte Carlo had
> betrayed her husband with a schoolboy, but her motive
> had been generous. Martha too had betrayed her hus-
> band but it was not Martha's love for me which held me,
> if she did love, it was her blind unselfish attachment to
> her child (*C*, pp. 129-130).

Brown realizes he had been attracted to his mistress because of
her special kind of virtue, which grew out of commitment and

offered a deep sense of security.

Although Brown feels a need for security at the beginning of the novel, he is seen to be returning to a land where only sudden violence can be expected with any certainty. In this novel Greene occasionally stretches the use of irony to the breaking point, and this may at first seem to be another example of what is the novel's one significant flaw. However, in this particular instance, the use of extreme irony has the proper effect. It makes us focus on the fact that, due to those submerged emotional ties which have already been suggested, Brown is drawn back to Haiti because it has become the nearest thing to home he knows. Besides, it urges us to comprehend Brown's view that Haiti is no worse than any other place, that it "was not an exception in a sane world: it was a small slice of everyday taken at random. Baron Samedi walked in all our graveyards" (*C*, p. 121). Papa Doc is a political demon whose spirit can be found wherever there is pain. As Brown says, "Cruelty's like a searchlight. It sweeps from one spot to another. We can only escape it for a time" (*C*, p. 154). The horror of our age is real, and, he feels sure at this point, there is nothing much one can do about it.

In this context, one of the passengers on board the ship taking Brown back to Papa Doc's dark country might seem particularly absurd at first. Mr. Smith is going to a land of grinding poverty with the utopian idea of setting up a vegetarian center. He is a dedicated advocate of the vegetarian diet because he is convinced it offers the surest means to a more ideal future. To him vegetarianism "isn't only a question of diet. . . . It touches life at many points. If we really eliminated acidity from the human body," he thinks, "we would eliminate passion" (*C*, p. 15). Brown wonders if with the end of passion the world would not cease altogether; but Mr. Smith's rejoinder that in referring to passion he did not mean love makes Brown feel ashamed of his cynicism. Because Mr. Smith has an unflinching belief in the strength of human affection, he eventually attains a towering dignity in the eyes of Brown.

At one point Brown does wonder whether it was not perhaps a "flaw in character to believe so passionately in the integrity of all the world" as does Mr. Smith (*C*, p. 152). Mr. Smith's extravagant faith in humanity is, after all, often challenged by terrible events. There are times when he can appear absurdly naive about the motives of political gangsters. But if Mr. Smith can be fooled, it is only for a period of time; he is never defeated by deception because he instinctively travels to the core of the human heart. Since he is guided by a compassionate vision, he rises against the fears of his time like a mythical hero. All this Brown ultimately learns to understand about Mr. Smith, so that toward the end of the novel he has some thoughts about the man he once believed to be comical which reveal the form of his affection and desire:

> He was an old man with beautiful manners, and suddenly I realized how much I missed him. In the school-chapel at Monte Carlo we prayed every Sunday, "*Dona nobis pacem,*" but I doubt whether that prayer was answered for many in the life that followed. Mr. Smith had no need to pray for peace. He had been born with peace in his heart instead of the splinter of ice (*C,* p. 235).

Brown is convinced that he and Mr. Smith are still continents apart. Nevertheless, because his nostalgia is so fervid, his cold self-analysis is not entirely convincing.

Jones, another passenger aboard the ship bound for Haiti, at first appears to Brown to be a complete contrast to Mr. Smith. Indeed in many ways this is true. Jones is certainly not going to Haiti for any idealistic purpose; what brings him is a plan to make a quick fortune on a shady deal. He is not naive about man's capacity for betrayal; mendacity has been the way of his life. Furthermore, if he gives the impression of composure, it is largely an act at those times when he feels most lost within himself. In the end, however, he will find peace in his heart because in a primary way he is like Mr. Smith. He, too, has the gift of child-like innocence which allows him to commit himself to a cause. Moreover, he has learned to combat the desolation of his age with the "trick of laughter" (*C,* p. 141). Because he is able to laugh at the sad comedy of life and to make others laugh with him, he is a "good comedian" whose act forms a relief to the gayety of despair.

At the beginning of the novel when Brown considers the names of Smith and Jones in combination with his own, it occurs to him that they appear "interchangeable like comic masks in a farce" (*C,* p. 17). Then as he becomes engaged in their lives, he changes his attitude. While his imagination awakens to their individual characters, he discovers he has been wrong in his assumption that they were rather droll caricatures.

We have already seen how his estimation of Mr. Smith grew, until Brown thought of him in terms of a father figure. As for
Jones, he at first suggests a kind of mirror image of his own contorted self to Brown. Later, as Jones' image straightens in his
mind, Brown begins to look on him as a counterpart who sym-
bolizes what he has lost. This becomes clear during the night
when Jones calls upon Brown to help him escape from revengeful
Haitian authorities whom he had tried to trick in a fraudulent
scheme. It's then Brown has a significant dream:

> I fell asleep and dreamt I was a boy kneeling at the com-
> munion-rail in the college chapel in Monte Carlo. The
> priest came down the row and placed in each mouth a
> bourbon biscuit, but when he came to me he passed me
> by. The communicants on either side came and went
> away, but I knelt obstinately on. Again the priest dis-
> tributed the biscuits and left me out. I stood up then and
> walked sullenly away down the aisle, which had become
> an immense aviary where parrots stood in ranks chained
> to their crosses. Someone called out sharply behind me,
> "Brown, Brown," but I was not certain whether that was
> my name or not, for I didn't turn. "Brown." This time
> I awoke and a voice came up to me from the verandah be-
> low my room (*C*, p. 187).

The dream shows once again how intensely Brown feels the de-
privation of his faith and the condition of his abandonment. He
will answer the call of Jones, though, and as a result a different
prospect will eventually appear.

At this point Brown is willing to be of help perhaps primarily because he has a natural inclination to side with what
Jones calls the "tarts."[29] However, when Brown winds up leaving him in the house of Martha and her ambassador husband in
a state of political assylum for a seeminly interminable period,
he becomes increasingly suspicious of the relations between his
mistress and Jones. So when he once more helps Jones to escape,
this time in order to join a miserable little band of rebels, Brown
is motivated by jealousy. Then, during the course of this flight,
something strange happens to him:

> It was like meeting an unknown brother—Jones and
> Brown, the names were almost interchangeable, and so

was our status. For all we knew we were both bastards, although of course there might have been a ceremony—my mother had always given me that impression. We had both been thrown into the water to sink or swim, and swim we did—we had swum from very far apart to come together in a cemetery in Haiti. "I like you, Jones," I said (*C,* pp. 254-255).

Brown begins to understand that he has been wrong about Jones all along. He had heard Jones describe his dream of owning a luxurious golf club, and so he had dismissed him as a small-time gambler who played at gin rummy but had extravagant tastes. Now he is surprised to discover that the golf club was merely the second dream of Jones. His first dream, it turns out, is to belong to something of permanent significance, to find a "good place." It begins to dawn on Brown that Jones had "perhaps in all his devious life . . . been engaged on a secret and hopeless love-affair with virtue, watching virtue from a distance, hoping to be noticed, perhaps, like a child doing wrong in order to attract the attention of virtue" (*C,* p. 255).

By joining the insurgents, Jones fulfills his primary dream in an unexpected way. The small band is doomed to fail in its effort to start a revolution against Papa Doc. Still, it offers Jones an opportunity for commitment that saves him from absurdity. He dies, of course, yet he becomes a kind of saint to his followers, and even perhaps to Brown. They erect a stone to commemorate him, and Brown, whenever he passes the modest monument, finds no reason to mock it. Instead, he feels a "certain pride" that his "action helped to raise it" (*C,* p. 3). In expressing a view shared by several of the novel's other critics, C. H. Muller wrote that Brown "undergoes no regeneration whatsoever; at the close of the novel he feels neither love nor guilt. . . . The final impression is one of total failure."[30] The thrust of the story, however, doesn't really bear out this conclusion. Actually, Brown's final attitude toward Jones, which incidentally is made apparent in the first paragraph of the novel as if to suggest a new beginning, clearly reveals that Brown has undergone some significant change. The second paragraph of the novel begins with Brown's statement that there exists "a point of no return unremarked at the time in most lives" (*C,* p. 3). What this thought finally means is that while Brown begins to get involved in the lives of Smith and Jones in particular, he crosses over from the region of egoistical exclusion into a different sphere. As his imagination comes alive, he envisions the true nature of Smith and Jones, among others, and expresses his admiration for them in a paradoxical fashion by writing a book-length confession which analyzes his own flaws and commemorates their virtues.

The most monumental figure in this testimonial is that of Dr. Magiot. Towering in his strength and virtue, he leaves a permanent impression on the imagination of Brown. No other character proliferates into so many roles in the mind of Brown. Superbly, he rises out of the torments of Haiti and Brown's memory to assume the roles of Papa Doc's antithesis and Brown's spiritual doctor, father-figure, and secular priest. Guided by a vision of compassion, he is archetypical of the truly involved man. Furthermore, in being guided by real virtue, he also has a choric function, isolating truth from falsehood and putting events into perspective.

Consequently, when Brown hears of Dr. Magiot's death, he feels momentarily lost, experiencing "for the first time the sense of sudden separation from someone on whom as a last resort [he] could depend" (*C,* p. 273). Nevertheless, because Dr. Magiot leaves a legacy in the form of a letter behind, Brown's despair is suspended as he is urged toward a hopeful direction:

> We are humanists, you and I. You won't admit it perhaps, but you are the son of your mother and you once took that dangerous journey which we all have to take before the end. Catholics and Communists have committed great crimes, but at least they have not stood aside, like an established society, and been indifferent. I would rather have blood on my hands than water like Pilate. I know you and love you well, and I am writing this letter with some care because it may be the last chance I have of communicating with you. . . . I implore you . . . if you have abandoned one faith, do not abandon all faith. There is always an alternative to the faith we lose. Or is it the same faith under another mask (*C,* pp. 274-275)?

In other words, the varieties of faiths one can find are masks for a commitment to life essentially unified by a "service to man."[31]

Brown's first impulse is to believe that Dr. Magiot's advice has come too late, but the letter prompts a final dream which suggests that his self-doubt is a form of emerging faith. He dreams of Jones, who

> lay among the dry rocks on the flat plain beside me and he said, "Don't ask me to find water. I can't. I'm tired, Brown, tired. After the seven hundredth performance I sometimes dry up on my lines—and I've only two lines."
> I said to him, "Why are you dying, Jones?"
> "It's in my part, old man, it's in my part. But I've got this comic line—you should hear the whole theatre laugh when I say it. The ladies in particular."
> "What is it?"
> "That's the trouble. I've forgotten it."
> "Jones, you must remember."
> "I've got it now. I have to say—just look at these bloody rocks—'This is a good place,' and everyone laughs till the tears come. Then you say, 'To hold the bastards up?' and I reply, 'I didn't mean that' " (*C*, p. 275).

Jones' answer to Brown's urgent entreaty might appear to be ambiguous at first, until it becomes clear that Jones meant literally what he said. Jones had found "a good place," not one which merely holds up "the bastards" but which serves as a shrine because of his final commitment to it in the form of a sacrificial death.

Since Brown is not the type to die for a country, a lover, or an idea, he is not sure whether he is capable of deep feeling. Just prior to his discovery that Jones has died and his little band mauled, Brown takes a long look at himself and decides that perhaps his life of dislocation is quite likely an advantage after all. Without roots, he tells himself,

> one accepts more easily what comes. The rootless have experienced, like all the others, the temptation of sharing the security of a religious creed or a political faith, and for some reason we have turned the temptation down. We are the faithless; we admire the dedicated, the Doctor Magiots and the Mr. Smiths, for their courage and their integrity, for their fidelity to a cause, but through timidity, or through lack of sufficient zest, we find ourselves the only ones truly committed—committed to the whole world of evil and of good, to the wise and to the foolish,

> to the indifferent and to the mistaken. We have chosen
> nothing except to go on living . . . (*C*, p. 268).

Then, however, he immediately indicates that he realizes this is merely an "argument" which interests him and serves to ease his "never quiet conscience" (*C*, p. 268).

It's because he does have a conscience that he becomes a mourner of those who have died as a result of their engagement against the political demons who terrify Haiti. That is why it is fitting he should become the partner of Mr. Fernandez, an undertaker, at the end of this violent story.

In this novel where indifference is the worst fault, there are various forms in which love may be expressed.[32]   Brown's happens to be the most quaint and ambiguous. He becomes an undertaker because this position represents "a good place" for one having come to the understanding that death is a mark of sincerity and for one wishing to make penance for past insincerities by mourning the victims of life.

Early in the novel, before the ship arrives in Port-au-Prince, a farewell concert is given for the passengers. The entertainment has the quality of high farce, and the absurdity is heightened by the decoration of French letters blown up and painted over with comic faces. During the course of the droll celebration, Mr. Fernandez suddenly breaks into tears. We eventually learn that a personal sadness was on his mind, but the immediate impression left is that life is an extreme comedy which brings out the tears. Brown is never seen to literally weep. On the other hand, his written testament is filled with restrained sorrow. And because, as he says, he can laugh on his best days, he is not the hollow man he himself might have thought.

Finally, there remains the impression of one apparently passing incident which indicates better than any other the form of Brown's salvation. During a brief visit with Martha's son, he is challenged by the child to solve a puzzle:

> It was one of those little rectangular boxes with glass sides
> that contain a picture of a clown and two sockets where
> his eyes should be and two little beads of steel which
> have to be shaken into the holes. I turned it this way and
> that way; I would get one bead in place and then in trying
> to fix the other I would dislodge the first (*C*, p. 127).

The image of the puzzle serves perfectly to represent Brown's attempt to solve the complexity of life. The problem is he does not for a long time look at things steadily. His constant movement dislodges first one, then another vision or belief. Therefore, Brown will remain the blind clown, unless he can find a "trick." The hideous child, ironically named Angel, has a concealed little magnet which pulls the mercury into the eye sockets. Such self-deception in real life would obviously only prolong one's blindness. The point, though, has been made—a "trick" which draws the vision into focus is necessary before the clown can see. In the course of his story Brown in fact comes upon several "tricks" which allow various people to have a clear vision. Then, upon learning to comprehend the real gravity of his mother, Martha, Mr. Smith, Jones, and Dr. Magiot, and others, he finds his own way. Thus the form of the novel is essentially that of a mystery which is continuously tilted in different directions, until the vision of the narrator is complete and the picture of the sad clown is made clear to the reader who is challenged to respond with sympathetic identification.

Travels With My Aunt

During the year when *The Comedians* was published, Greene was at work on a series of short stories which were subsequently collected in a volume entitled *May We Borrow Your Husband?* (1967). It's safe to say that none of these stories is in itself indispensable to an understanding of Greene and his art. The book as a whole, however, is significant in one important way, and this has to do with its general mood. As in the preceding three novels, the comic approach in *May We Borrow Your Husband?* predominates, except that now the mood is much less somber. In fact, it's one of outright hilarity.[33] Greene has speculated that he was in such a mood at the time because of two personal factors. He was in a state of exhilaration while setting up a new home in Antibes, and he had discovered laughter as a means of escape from the thought of his death during what he then believed would be his last decade of life.[34] Without in any way discounting these factors, it should be pointed out that behind this mood of gayety there also existed aesthetic and philosophical impulses. When put in chronological perspective, it becomes clear that these humorous short stories were the natural outgrowth of the comic direction his art had been following in the preceding novels. Moreover, it eventually became clear that these stories were not just a drifting continuation of Greene's attempt to envision the world in a comic vein, but actually a kind of warm-up for *Travels With My Aunt* (1969), the novel which culminates Greene's comic phase.

When *Travels With My Aunt* came out, it was met with a great deal of applaus but little understanding. Most reviewers praised it for the pure fun it provided, and then, like the critic Haskel Frankel, tended to dismiss it as a "soufflé of a novel" which didn't really warrant a rigorous examination.[35] This was a mistake. Greene has said that *Travels With My Aunt* was the only book he has ever written "for the fun of it," and that as he was writing the story he didn't know from day to day where it was going, feeling in the process "like a dreamer who watches his dream unfold without power to alter its course."[36] This carefree nonchalance was no doubt responsible for some of the flaws which can be discerned in the novel, such flaws as an extremely loose plot structure and a tendency to indulge in private, nostalgic allusions. Nevertheless, a serious analysis of the novel also reveals that the story has far more substance than its critics were prone to give it credit for, and that indeed it represents an effulgent statement of Greene's final form of comic salvation—personal vitalism.

In turning from the kind of comedy found in *The Comedians* to that found in *Travels With My Aunt*, one is bound to be struck by the adjustments in the nature of the laughter and the ways of the protagonist. The predominant tone in *The Comedians* was lugubrious and sardonic. In *Travels With My Aunt*, it's one of audacious gayety, so vigorous that it grows into a lusty song of affirmation. In *The Comedians* the protagonist learns to look upon life as a sad comedy, and because he becomes a sympathetic mourner of its participants, he is saved from the egoistical exclusion which brings about the condition of personal decay. Henry Pulling, the narrator and focal character of *Travels With My Aunt*, who is similarly in the process of wasting away in the isolation of his world, is saved in a different way. At the beginning of the novel, Henry is entering his final years without ever having actually lived, and indeed he appears ready for a premature burial. But he escapes the condition of meaningless existence by learning he must breach the prison of the passing years of unrelieved dullness through the accumulated strength of vibrant memories and the energy of youthful imagination. By ultimately choosing to surrender the monotonous security of his old life which amounts to a form of nonexistence and by bursting into the dangerous but vivid turbulence of the contemporary world, he goes through an essential transformation.

What happens to Pulling (as the sound of his name nearly suggests) is that he changes from a cold egg to a quaint chicken and finally is transmogrified into a rooster of sorts. At the start of the novel, he is really a cold egg. For one thing, he seems extremely hard to crack since he has been inside his shell for a half century. As it turns out, he has simply been in need of motherly attention all this time. Still, in a bit of necessary transfiguration because Henry is also a human being, it takes some nine more months after the arrival of the mother for her reluctant offspring to break out completely into the light of day. If Henry seems unusually loath to be born, it's because he is quite certain he is happy in the obscurity of his little world. Since he cannot see the brilliant world outside his prison, he is content to remain in the dark security of his ignorance. Fortunately, the shell will crack, because the mother pecks at it persistently, or because it travels under her wing through a world full of violent agitation. And since (in the final metaphorical sense) Henry blinks at the hard light of reality not with fear but with curiosity and joy, and looks about him with childlike wonder, he experiences a radical re-birth.

When we first see Henry, he is a lifeless bachelor who has retired from the banking business to lead a conditioned, careful, inert existence. He is past the meridian of his life, but he has little to show for it, least of all lively memories. He is fond of recalling he was rewarded with a "silver handshake" upon retirement and that he was occasionally asked to dine with Sir Alfred Keene and his somber daughter, for example. As for his present life, he is proud of raising dahlias and becomes agreeably excited by the prospect of a funeral. If he has any worries, they are mainly about his dahlias getting enough water or his lawnmower rusting if it is left out in the rain. He has, as he says, an adequate pension, because he has no extravagances. The nearest he comes to being daring with his money is when he orders a meal to be catered by Chicken.

Henry believes there is nothing more worthwhile in life than security, but he discovers just how boring and insipid his existence has actually been with the appearance of Aunt Augusta at the funeral of his ostensible mother. When she arrives, Henry is as ready for the fire as the body which he has brought to the crematorium. Fortunately, he is saved from his living death by beginning to travel with Aunt Augusta and to listen to her stories about intense love and resourceful struggles with death.

These trips and stories add up to a successful education in the ways of breaking out of a world dominated by arbitrary power, deep skepticism, and meaningless death. Basically, they indicate that life is absurd if one is carried along by the tides of the modern age, and that even death cannot attain the element of tragedy since it is merely the end of a pointless career. They also show that if one has sufficient imagination, he can transform life into a comedy where the auhority is the buffoon, the skeptic is the fool, and death is a state of mind.

The element of farce is particularly strong in the early part of the story because Henry was then largely a caricature of a human being. Because his mind had been captured by the idea of respectability, he resembled a type of person who merely imitates life. If he had any thoughts and beliefs, they were the reflections of what was safely accepted. Afraid of the world because he had not discovered the energy of imagination, he paradoxically thought to save himself by surrendering to its indifferent power.

Although Henry takes only formulated authority seriously at first, he eventually learns to take individuals seriously, and finally even himself. When he learns to think of himself not as a citizen loyal to the institutions of his country but as a human being loyal to other human beings, he assumes a gravity which saves him from being a mere caricature. At the same time, because he can subsequently tell his story with self-deprecating humor, he indicates he is not the slave of his ego. Having learned to laugh at himself, he can laugh at the whole spectacle of life and thus transform it into a comedy. He can then recognize his own absurdity; however, this is no reason for despair. This insight becomes instead the source of a new life for Henry. Intrigue, surprise, paradox, and nonsense are desirous in life because they provide an extra dimension of interest. Man may still be a clown, but with the discovery that imagination is theanthropic, he can create his own act.

All this is what one finds by following Henry's picaresque story of self-discovery. As Henry goes further afield, he also goes deeper and deeper into himself, until he finds that *he* can be his own entrapping or liberating genius. When that understanding is complete, so is his salvation. Not being pagan like a Zorba the Greek character, Henry's understanding does not come to him through instinct. He is the civilized, not the natural, man who has to go through a process of rational analysis before conviction follows. Consequently, because each step of his mental journey indicates the measure not only of his self-awareness but also of the success of his imagination in subduing the rational demands within him, it is important to follow Henry's story in sequence. Besides, if the story is analyzed in this manner, it becomes clear that its climacteric points serve to highlight a code which, Greene suggests, can guide one is a secular world.

The first journey with Aunt Augusta is the shortest but, as he eventually realizes, perhaps the most memorable of the several they are going to make together. Even though it is only to her apartment, Henry's old view of life is thoroughly confounded during this short adventure.

Henry has prided himself on belonging to the respectable class of society. Now he is suddenly confronted with an indication by Aunt Augusta that he might be a bastard child. Although he has always tried to control his emotion, this surprise is great enough to give him a good case of the hiccups. His notion of ancestral respectability is further shaken when he discovers that Aunt Augusta has a black lover. Henry cannot at first grasp the possibility that Wordsworth is much more than a loyal servant, because Aunt Augusta is after all some seventy years old. However, she has not been defeated by time, Henry soon finds out. She can still surprise the world with her vital energy because she believes intensely what she tells Henry, that age "may a little modify our emotions—it does not destroy them."[37] With her "brilliant red hair, monumentally piled," her "two big front teeth which gave her a vital Neanderthal air," and her "sea-deep blue eyes" that look forward with relish to new adventure, she still exerts a powerful attraction (*TWMA*, pp. 4-5).

Besides her sensual appeal, there is a more beguiling one. She bewitches certain persons who come in contact with her because there is something utterly magical about her. When Henry first enters her apartment, he is dazzled by its brillance:

> The lights were on in the living-room, now that the day
> had darkened, and my eyes were dazzled for a moment

by rays from the glass ornaments which flashed back from
every open space. There were angels on the buffet wearing robes striped like peppermint rock; and in an alcove
there was a Madonna with a gold face and a gold halo and
a blue robe. On a sideboard on a gold stand stood a navy-
blue goblet, large enough to hold at least four bottles of
wine, with a gold trellis curled around the bowl on which
pink roses grew and green ivy. There were mauve storks
on the bookshelves and red swans and blue fish. Black
girls in scarlet dresses held green candle sconces, and
shining down on all this was a chandelier which might
have been made of sugar icing hung with pale-blue, pink,
and yellow blossoms (*TWMA*, p. 12).

Aunt Augusta's place serves as a concrete extension of her essential being. Because her imagination is vivid, the world to her
is full of brilliant color and exquisite beauty. She is an en-
chantress in a world of grace. Like her Venetian art objects,
though, she has to be cast in the proper light or she will appear
merely glossy, transparent, and cheap. Initially, Henry looks
upon Aunt Augusta's glass collection, and on her life, as being
"not in the best of taste" (*TWMA*, p. 12). When he begins to
comprehend her animating charm, he starts to leave his somber
notions behind, and even forgets the package holding the ashes
of his supposed mother as he leaves for his home. The ashes
are adulterated with Cannabis before he is able to retrieve them;
and beginning with this brief journey to her aparmtnet, Henry's
life will be imbued with the never quite reputable but always provocative element of Aunt Augusta.

The next trip for Henry in the company of Aunt Augusta is
still of only slight geographical distance. Nevertheless, when they
go to Brighton, where Henry hopes to spend a quiet little holiday
revisiting favorite old places, he actually undergoes a mental
voyage which takes him a long way into a new world.[38]

In Brighton Henry has his fortune read by Hatty, an old
friend of Aunt Augusta, who informs him that according to the
tea leaves he is going to do a great deal of traveling with a female
friend in the future. Henry is skeptical about such a prediction
because, after all, he considers it quite daring of him to have
traveled even as far as Brighton. Besides, superstition has no
place in his still thoroughly rational world. But he will discover
before too long that, if the imagination is sufficiently alive, then

the "leaves don't lie" (*TWMA*, p. 34).

Aunt Augusta, of course, trusts the leaves because she has faith in the irrational and because she has been "interested in religion . . . ever since Curran" (*TMWA*, p. 34). Curran, one of her very first lovers, established a church in Brighton which had a most bizarre congregation—dogs. In his own peculiar way, he indicated that he was a truly religious man who understood that, given a merciful God, "dogs and sorcerers and whoremongers and murderers and idolaters and whoever loveth or maketh a lie" might be saved because "they all have souls" and that, consequently, they "only have to repent" to be allowed to enter the gates of heaven (*TWMA*, p. 38).

Originally, Aunt Augusta was dubious about Curran's "dogs" and the society they are believed to keep, and so she could not forsee their possible salvation. Nor could she then comprehend that she and Curran actually belonged to such a company—although Curran was more precisely an elephant in the sense that he was of the type which "never changes his mate and . . . tenderly loves the one of his choice" (*TWMA*, p. 40). Being very young and hence rather self-centered and suspicious of Curran's attentions, Aunt Augusta lost him. Yet she has retained the memories of his true fidelity which she now understands and of his strange ability to communicate with animals. In a novel which sometimes assumes the guise of a beast fable, the resonance of Curran's simple sermons of love reverberates continuously. It's a theme which quickly captures the imagination of Henry, so that when he begins to review what has occurred to him since has has met Aunt Augusta and considers the story of Curran which she has just told him, he "had a sense of fear and exhilaration too, as the music pounded from the Pier and the phosphorescence rolled up the beach" (*TWMA*, p. 41).

The force of Aunt Augusta is entering his life, but Henry still reacts with fear. He is certain that if he surrenders to her power, he will find excitement but also mortal danger. After all, death is a recurring theme in the story of her life. But death, as he learns from her, need not be meaningless even if it comes suddenly and seems painfully farcical at times. As a matter of fact, if one converges upon death with daring, he might experience a remarkable form of perpetuation. To defeat time, what one needs is a vivid imagination and creative energy. Aunt Augusta seems immortal because she means to explore the limits of her mortality, just like her Uncle Jo, as she recalls, challenged the limits of his last days.

Uncle Jo decided to retire from bookmaking in order to take the extended world tour he had long dreamed of. Before he really got far along, however, he had a serious heart attack. Nevertheless, he decided if he could not travel physically, he would do so mentally. Thus he bought a crumbling Italian *palazzo* and had it restored and partitioned into fifty-two rooms, including the kitchen, bathroom, and lavatory. The idea was to imitate a world voyage by going from room to room, week by week, with the w.c. saved as the last place. Uncle Jo's mental journey was quite successful for almost a year. Then he had his second stroke in the fifty-first room. His travels appeared to be over for good, since he was now partially paralyzed. However, one day, gathering himself with terrific effort, he started out to crawl toward the w.c. while pulling his suitcase tied to a tie with him. He died before he arrived at the final room, but to Aunt Augusta his end does not really seem pathetic. She is saddened by the memory of Uncle Jo lying on the tiles, panting and making "a little pool of wee-wee" (*TWMA*, p. 52). Yet she understands he was relieved to have made the effort; by straining to reach the last resting place, he saved himself from a more awful end. She knows he has had a full life because, as he told her, grinning, the final trip seemed to him "like a whole lifetime" (*TWMA*, p. 52). To Aunt Augusta there is no better way to die than in passage. As she well knows, a good life is not the result of the gathering of years but of memories; and travel is the best means of accumulating adventures one will later be pleased to recall.

The story of Uncle Jo affects Henry deeply. He is not quite certain that Aunt Augusta has not embellished the story; however, unlike his former self, he thinks: "What did the truth matter? All characters once dead, if they continue to exist in memory at all, tend to become fiction" (*TWMA*, p. 53). It is the imagination which alone can give deathless life, he is beginning to understand.

Nonetheless, Henry still has a long way to go before his natal education is complete. During the next trip with Aunt Augusta, this time to Istanbul, he learns a number of other essential lessons which explain her joy of living. Reacting like the conscientious banker he was, Henry finds fault with the improvidence of Aunt Augusta. He still values being prudent and cautious, considering them to be the sterling qualities which made Britain great. As far as Aunt Augusta is concerned, such an attitude makes Henry seem mean and hard instead of commendable. She believes in the most lavish pleasure she can afford, and even more so at her present age because, she has concluded from years of experience, it is in middle age one truly begins to enjoy the sensual delights of life. Henry has always been frugal, for what good reason he would he hard pressed to explain. What he will now begin to learn is that, in the words of Aunt Augusta, "You must surrender yourself first to extravagance. . . . Poverty is apt to strike suddenly like influenza, it is well to have a few memories of extravagance in store for bad times" (*TWMA*, p. 62).

Above all, Henry must learn to surrender himself to the extravagance of love like Aunt Augusta. She had had many affairs, and because she has been able to give herselt to her partners with generosity and without calculation, their memories come back to enrich her life. When she recalls her affair with Dambreuse, she can weep with sad pleasure. Henry thinks the bizarre arrangement which amounted to Dambreuse's juggling two mistresses in two different wings of the same hotel without their or his wife's knowledge was a disgrace. Just as Aunt Augusta suspected before she started to tell him the story, he fails to recognize the humor of the situation. Moreover, she finds out to her fury, he cannot accept her willingness to have continued the arrangement after Dambreuse' splendid secret got out into the open. What Henry has to learn is that the region of love must be entered with abandon.

If one enters into love, he will find himself in a state of anarchy; but he will also find a way of salvation, because here he can be rescued from the absurdity of an egoistical life of calculation. Beginning to realize all this, Henry surprises himself with the discovery that dahlias are perhaps not a sufficient love in life after all. Following an impulse for the first time in memory, he blurts out, "I'm glad to have found you, Aunt Augusta" (*TWMA*, p. 75). And when she replies that there is plenty of life left in her "with a smile so speculative, so carefree and youthful," he is no longer surprised by the fact such younger men as Wordsworth could be jealous of her (*TWMA*, p. 75). Henry is beginning to truly understand that, in a sense, the old girl is an apotheosis of regenerating love.

A young girl whom Henry meets during the journey to Istanbul is, like Aunt Augusta, a life-giver because of her comparable ability to surrender herself freely. Tooley "turns on" Henry not merely because she innocently gets Henry to smoke marijuana but because she serves as an example of boundless loyalty. Julian, her boyfriend, may abuse her by acting rashly; but, like Aunt Augusta, she can accept without criticism those human failings based on passion. As Henry realizes when he sees her enormous watch with its great blank face and four bold numbers, in her life there is no time for petty irritations because she exists for the grander hours. She does not expend time and energy on the minor concerns which tend to consume Henry's life, and she certainly has no place in her life for hatred. Though very young in years, she could understand the wisdom of what Aunt Augusta tells Henry: "I despise no one. . . . Regret your own actions, if you like that kind of wallowing in self-pity, but never, never despise. Never presume yours is a bettery morality" (*TWMA,* p. 97).

When Henry finally returns from the trip to Istanbul, he is under the temporary illusion of having re-entered a happier world. Back at his home the atmosphere seems so much more civilized, with only an occasional Beatles' tune or a motorcycle interrupting his peace of mind. Now with great relief he can dial Chicken and order a decent British meal—cream of spinach soup, lamb cutlets, and cheddar cheese. Life seems idyllic for the moment. Then he finds out that his neighbor, Major Charge, believing in strict military discipline, has given the dahlias too little water. There is also a letter from Miss Keene, who now communicates her quiet sense of defeat from South Africa. Consequently, Henry's false impression of happiness is quickly dissipated, and he is left with a deep sense of depression he attempts to analyze:

> It was only too true that I was depressed: whether it was due to Miss Keene's letter or to the fact that I missed my aunt's company more than I had anticipated, or even that Tooley had left a blank behind her, I could not tell. Now that I had no responsibilities to anyone but myself, the pleasure of finding again my house and garden had begun to fade (*TWMA,* p. 127).

What he is forced to face up to in his isolation is that attachment to people, not to a certain place, is what really matters. Therefore, when his next opportunity to be the companion of Aunt Augusta arrives, he is quite ready to leave for new adventures.

This time the two companions go to Boulogne in order to

visit the grave of Henry's father. Although this trip across the English channel is a short one, Henry goes a long way toward acquiring the full knowledge of love which resides in the heart of Aunt Augusta. He has been an observant student of her love since he started traveling in the company of her wisdom. What he has yet to learn is that human love, if it becomes angelic, is fatal. To illustrate this point, Aunt Augusta tells him the story of William Curlew, the business partner of Henry's father. He had a wife who was sweet, good-natured, and efficient. In short, she was apparently without a flaw, even if she made rather large sexual demands on her husband. William, finding it too much of a strain to live with such a faultless wife, decided he had to leave her. But how does one desert an "angel?" Being more imaginative than his partner, Henry's father suggested what appeared to be a wonderful plan. William was to write an anonymous letter to his wife in which he accused himself of infidelity. What woman would not toss out such a cheating husband? The plan did not work, however, for this was no ordinary woman. She was the kind which is very content to forgive anything. As a result, poor William simply gave up. There remained no hope; she "was a perfect wife, uncrackably perfect" (*TWMA*, p. 134). Thus the word "perfect" tolled in William's ears like a signal for execution for the rest of his life, until he died in her arms, smothered by her sentimental affection.

Knowing that pity and piety are corrupt forms of love, Aunt Augusta is particularly hard on Miss Paterson, the little old woman who is discovered in an attitude of prayer at the grave of Henry's father. Aunt Augusta's motives for disapproval might appear to be mixed with jealousy, since we come to find out she loved Henry's father. Nevertheless, the more fundamental reason why she lashes out at Miss Paterson is because of her resemblance to William's wife. Aunt Augusta believes that she, too, is the kind of woman who, because of her maudlin affection, stifles passion. Therefore, Aunt Augusta holds her in great part responsible for the death of Henry's father. Henry, still retaining some of that somber romanticism which appears gothic at times, comes to the defense of Miss Paterson. Unlike Aunt Augusta, he thinks the end of his father—whispering "Dolly, my darling," and then expiring with his head in her lap—is romantic. He is touched by her long and severe loyalty to his father's memory, and consequently he believes she has *really* loved him. Aunt Augusta, on the other hand, realizes there is something too morbid about Miss Paterson's fidelity, and thus she dismisses her as just a "little sentimental creature" (*TWMA,* p. 143). Aunt Augusta has the capacity for great loyalty, but only for the living, not for the dead and their graves. Because her treatment of Miss Paterson challenges Henry's vision of what true love is like, he reacts with anger at first. Later, in a more contemplative frame of mind, he realizes that perhaps she had good reason to feel contempt for Miss Paterson after all:

> I thought of Curran and Monsieur Dambreuse and Mr. Visconti—they lived in my imagination as though she had actually created them: even poor Uncle Jo struggling towards the lavatory. She was one of the life-givers. Even Miss Paterson had come to life, stung by the cruelty of her questions (*TWMA,* p. 143).

After the trip to Boulogne, Aunt Augusta disappears from Henry's life for several months; thus he is suddenly left with what he calls an "empty time" (*TWMA,* p. 170). She has disturbed his old life sufficiently so that he cannot return to it. By entering her world, he has discovered the enchantment of unexpected adventure. Above all, he has started truly to comprehend the magical power of Aunt Augusta's imaginative love. In fact, he himself begins now to reveal such a creative form of love for Aunt Augusta in his thoughts, although the term he still uses might be "loyalty":

> All my working life I had been strictly loyal to one establishment, the bank, but my loyalty now was drawn in quite another direction. Loyalty to a person inevitably entails loyalty to all the imperfections of a human being, even to the chicanery and immorality from which my aunt was not entirely free. I wondered whether she had ever forged a cheque or robbed a bank, and I smiled at the thought with the tenderness I might have shown in the past to a small eccentricity (*TWMA,* p. 160).

This smile of tolerance is a measure of just how far he has become engaged in the vision of Aunt Augusta. Consequently, when he finally receives a brief letter from her commanding him to join her in South America, Henry does not hesitate to go because he knows full well that his life depends on it.

To demonstrate that Henry has matured to the point where he can make the ultimate decision to break away from the fatality of his past existence, Greene sets him out alone on this longest of his journeys. Moreover, by employing a two-part structure in the novel, Greene emphasizes that Henry is finally breaking out of his protective shell. In the first part Henry has been seen groping about, lost, managing to find his way only with the guidance of Aunt Augusta. In the second part, he leaves his former circumscribed existence behind and enters her world with a clear vision.

Henry can now see, for example, why a Czech fellow passenger on the ship bound for Paraguay is so content with his present life. He had suffered terribly because of Nazi brutality; but he has put those past horrors behind him, and has since been simply happy to be alive and free. Moreover, Henry can now feel that Tooley's father, who is coincidentally another fellow passenger, is not as absurd as he might initially appear. It seems at first that he has one prominent ambition in life, to record as accurately as possible the amount of time he spends urinating. What saves him from inanity is his dedication to his daughter. When one has such a deep sense of responsibility, his life does not go down the drain.

Most important, Henry is finally able to understand himself clearly. In a long dialogue with himself, he demonstrates that he fully realizes he has been going through a process of deliverance:

> . . . I thought of my home in Southwood, of my garden, of Major Charge trumpeting across the fence, and of the sweet sound of the bells from Church Road. But I remembered Southwood now with a kind of friendly tolerance. . . , the place where I myself no longer belonged. It was as though I had escaped from an open prison, had been snatched away, provided with a rope ladder and a waiting car, into my aunt's world, the world of the unexpected character and the unforseen event. There the rabbit-faced smuggler was at home, the Czech with his two million plastic straws, and poor O'Toole busy making a record of his urine (*TWMA*, p. 185).

Perhaps, he theorizes, his trap was formed early in his life through the passionless books he then read. In any case, he realizes he had missed the vision of magnificent passion which has made such a free and noble spirit of Aunt Augusta. She had attained a kind of immortality, while he had been merely moral. It may be, he concludes, that such "a sense of morality is the sad compensation we learn to enjoy, like a remission for good conduct" (*TWMA,* p. 186). Certainly, in the vision of Aunt Augusta there is no "morality." "I had been born as a result of what my stepmother would have called an immoral act, an act of darkness," he now admits to himself. "I had begun in immoral freedom. Why then should I have found myself in a prisonhouse? My real mother had certainly not been imprisoned anywhere" (*TWMA,* p. 186). Because he can face his dark lineage so directly, he is right to think to himself: "I have escaped" (*TWMA,* p. 186).

His gestation period now over, Henry emerges into the dangerous, primitive, vivid world of Aunt Augusta—not surprisingly, the kind of world which one tends to find in Greene's other novels. Starting his spatial and emotional journey without maps as an orphan, Henry finally crosses the border into the region where he finds both parents and a real home. The name of this new home, Asuncion, is paradoxical in the sense that it is the capital of a land of sudden death which is dominated by a political demon. But it is also a place of religious innocence which seems more often than not strangely edenic. In this garden spot of blooming flowers and fruit trees, it is the experienced, however, who survive by deceiving the demon.

The most experienced persons in this territory are Aunt Augusta and Visconti, who turn out to be the primal parents of this story. The reader has, of course, long been lead to suspect that Aunt Augusta is not only the spiritual but also the natural mother of Henry. As for Visconti, the man whom Aunt Augusta has loved above all others because she feels wonderfully free with him since he makes no claims upon her, he turns out to be a surprisingly natural father figure.

In this initiation story, Henry has learned most of his lessons about life from his mother. There is one lesson, however, which Visconti teaches him even better than she can—that of survival. Visconti has had many close calls in his long career of mischief, but he has always managed to survive by using his wits, which generally meant going underground. In fact, he has gone underground so often that he has come to think of himself as a rat. This does not mean he has an attitude of self-abasement, for he has developed a great respect for rats. They are, as he says, "ahead of us indisputably in one respect—they live underground" (*TWMA*, p. 227). Given the violent condition of the present world, he concludes that the "future of the world lies with the rats" since they will be able to survive any surface catastrophes. All this does not mean that Visconti thinks very highly of mere security. On the contrary, he believes insecurity to be a "blessed state" (*TWMA*, p. 227). What is so admirable about a rat is that, living in a constant state of insecurity, he is forever challenged to prove he is the best rat. He does not hestitate to accept such a challenge, and when he finally becomes a casualty of his career, he goes to his death with a great sense of dignity. This is how Visconti sees the life of a rat, and thus he likes to think of himself as "an honorary rat" (*TWMA*, p. 228).

It may seem a little too absurd to suggest that such a rat, who is also often referred to as a viper, should be the father-figure of a chicken. In this wild world, though, transmutation is an important quality. If one can change, it's a sign of life. If one can assume the form of a beast, it's a sign he has the basic passion which is desired.

Because Visconti has the required vitality, he is a life-giver like Henry's mother. Therefore, it is fitting for the novel to end with a celebration at the center of which remains the image of Henry's mother and her aged lover "dancing a slow waltz . . . bound in the deep incurable egotism of passion" (*TWMA*, p. 243). Both have always had the necessary grace to take part in the dance of life. And when Henry finally joins them in that dance, too, the "family group" is complete (*TWMA*, p. 244).

Greene once made the comment that *Travels With My Aunt* "was a sad book about death that turned out to be funny."[39] We have seen that this does not mean Greene deserts the melancholy subject of facing death in the course of the novel. What does happen is that the story begins with a vision of death and moves irresistibly to a conclusion which amounts to an exultant celebration of life.[40] In the process, it also develops into a much more significant novel than Greene evidently thought it might become or most of his critics realized. This is to say that, despite its light surface quality, *Travels With My Aunt* winds up as Greene's most spontaneous and direct testimonial of many of his personal, affirmative values.

VI.
THE LATE NOVELS

Upon the publication of *Travels With My Aunt,* two assumptions about Greene quickly arose. Both appeared to make sense at first, but both eventually proved to be wrong. One assumption was that *Travels With My Aunt* signalled a "new" Greene. To many of his readers, Greene now appeared to turn to the subject of sex with a mellow, wry aspect which more nearly resembled the comic fiction of someone like Joyce Cary than that of his previous dark books. He seemed, in other words, to have come to terms with the bestial element in man to the point where he could actually smile at it. To what extent did this outlook represent a real change in Greene? There is no doubt that the years separating Greene's earliest books from this novel had taken some of the edge off his sharpest views. Yet the lineations of these views, grounded on the values of justice and mercy, remained essentially the same. If in *Travels With My Aunt* it appeared that Greene had suddenly grown more sympathetic and understanding of human failings, it was an illusion created by the comic subject and style of the novel itself. The truth is that Greene always wrote with great sympathy for his characters, unless they did not themselves have the required sympathy for other human beings. In fact, it's safe to say that he has exhibited a strong element of charitable romanticism all of his writing career, an element so powerful that it can sometimes threaten the reality, or believability, of the reflective picture he is always trying to present of the contemporary world. Thus, it's only because of the fanciful nature of the novel that *Travels With My Aunt* seems to be written by a "new" Greene. In actual fact, this was still the same writer pursuing his search for ways in which we could be redeemed. He had already found grace and forms of personal commitment, and now he arrived at the possibility of a personal vision which extends into an animating vitalism.

The other assumption which sprang up after *Travels With*

My Aunt came out was that with this story Greene had decided to wind up his novel writing.[1] This may have seemed a logical enough assumption, because it was difficult to imagine where Greene could wish to go from this highly personal novel which, on one level, could be read like a parodic review of his long career. Needless to say, Greene was far from through with fiction. After only a rather brief pause, he felt compelled to get back to novel writing. The productive phase which then followed eventually saw him turn out two of his finest full-length novels and two novellas which, it may be argued, are as flawless as anything Greene has written. How can one explain such an upsurge of creative energy from a writer now entering old age after a very long career? The best explanation appears to be that, although Greene had been writing for about half a century already, he still had something to say. And, as always, the most important thing he still felt compelled to write about was the ideology of salvation, even if finally this meant analyzing its inverse futilities or basing its possibility on the mystery of human hope.

The Honorary Consul

Of all his novels, Greene has on occasion pointed to *The Honorary Consul* (1973) as his favorite. Although one needn't necessarily agree with Greene, it's easy to see why he could feel this way. Like most of the book's reviewers, he was bound to feel that he had managed to express a combination of the various elements which by this time could be called quintessentially Greene's, and that he had done so almost flawlessly.

Unfortunately, the one time in *The Honorary Consul* when Greene's art doesn't work perfectly is at a crucial point, so that the flaw appears glaring. This is toward the end of the story when the protagonist finds himself discussing the nature of God with a disenchanted priest whose ideas on the subject are even more unorthodox than were those of the priest in *The Power and the Glory*. To emphasize the importance of this discussion, Greene decided to employ the same kind of technique he had often used for the crucial, methaphysically weighted scenes in previous works. This meant in effect freezing the action, pitting two characters who could embody (however paradoxically) the opposing values of the body and the soul in debate, and giving the whole scene a heightened intensity, mainly through the use of evocative dialogue. In *The Power and the Glory,* for example, this strategy worked exceedingly well. This was because such a formulaic scene as the one between the whiskey priest and the lieutenant could be perceived to arise inevitably out of the purposely melodramatic and metaphorical quality of the whole story. However, because *The Honorary Consul* is dominated by an ironic, obliquely realistic approach, the attempt to use this same kind of strategy for intensifying a crucial scene turned out to be a mistake. Instead of arising quite naturally out of its context, the scene between the protagonist and the priest comes out stiff and self-consciously profound.

Aside from that, however, the rest of *The Honorary Consul* finds Greene in top form. Certainly he never wrote a novel where he exhibited more facility with creating affecting characters, vividly authentic settings, or a more appropriately detached and ironic tone. As for the moral thrust of the story, with the exception of the problematic scene focusing on God's nature, he was as successful as he had ever been in this regard. This was due in no small part to the power of the condensed, paradoxical, yet forcefully direct style which he had developed over the years. Finally, though, the successful expression of his thematic purpose depended most of all on the carefully structured story which he invented.

Like several of Greene's previous novels, the plot is set up to revolve around a protagonist who at the beginning is in a moribund state. Dr. Eduardo Plarr is initially a cool, cynical, self-centered person who is bored with his existence because he has been committed to nothing of real importance. Then he becomes involved in a bizarre situation which shatters the empty peace of his life. Since he has had a father in prison across the border in Paraguay, some rebels from that suppressed land approach him about helping them in a political kidnaping. The idea is to abduct an American ambassador and hold him hostage to an exchange of political prisoners. Plarr gives in because his father is one of those prisoners bargained for, because he knows two of the rebels from childhood, and because he believes that nothing will come of the plan anyway since the plotters are such amateurs.

Since they are amateurs, they kidnap the wrong man, an honorary British consul. The kidnaping starts out on a note of farce, but it ends in appalling violence. Before the ordeal is over, four of the participants die, including Plarr.

The fact that Plarr dies is not an unqualified tragedy, however, since the form of his death becomes an indication he had learned to truly live. Prior to his involvement with the rebels, he was an exile on a continent of exiles, belonging to no country or human being, living alone with his carefully measured desires. He had moments when he had a faint sense of something lost or forgotten. Not being able to understand why his heart was in conflict with itself, however, he merely dismissed life as an absurdity. Then as the pressure of his last hours builds up to a terrible intensity, he is forced to face himself with full honesty, and consequently he discovers those feelings which can save a man from a hollow existence. Learning at the last to submit to the irrational demands of his heart, he dies a renewed man.

Before his violent death suddenly occurs, Plarr has time to learn that pain and fear are not merely medical and emotional problems. They are essential aspects of experience. He begins to understand that if one succeeds in conquering them, he has actually lost an important part of his humanity. Moreover, Plarr has time to realize he has deceived himself in believing life is bearable if one reduces it to rational terms where there is no room for guilt. He had thought that by eliminating guilt through a reliance on reason, he could consider himself a "simple man." But he learns the truth of what Leon, the politicized priest who is the leader of the small group of rebels, has to say about the complex mystery of human nature:

> I have never met a simple man. Not even in the confessional, though I used to sit there for hours on end. Man was not created simple. When I was a young priest, I used to try to understand what motives a man or woman had, what temptations and self-delusions. But I soon learned to give all that up, because there was never a straight answer. No one was simple enough to me to understand. In the end I would just say, "Three Our Fathers, Three Hail Marys. Go in peace."[2]

Although he had been certain of having completely disposed of religion, Plarr has time before his sudden death to discover that metaphysical faith is not after all an absurdity, and that perhaps its germ was still alive in him. He had been sure that if his Jesuit education had left in him one trace of the disease of belief in God, at least he had succeeded in isolating and keeping it under control. Having faith in reason, he is inclined to ridicule religion, particularly if it takes the exotic form of Leon's view that God is both good and evil and that God's evolution to complete goodness is tied to the evolution of man. Yet Plarr is ultimately constrained to face the fact he "can no longer mock a man for his beliefs, however absurd" (*HC,* p. 260). As he begins to realize that Leon's strength is sustained by a commitment to a metaphysical vision, he can only envy him. Thus he begins to imagine the possible existence of God, even if He might be "a great joker . . . who likes to give a twist to things" (*HC,* p. 280). Moreover, as his last hour approaches, Plarr answers the question of Charley (the kidnaped consul) of whether he believes in anything at all in a revealing way. His initial response is that he does not. Then, because "the personal truth was out between them," he "felt a curious need to speak with complete accuracy." Consequently he adds, "I don't think so" (*HC,* p. 286). This confession of doubt is, if not a clear statement of religious belief, at least an ambivalent expression of not only his fear but also of his desire concerning his belief in something beyond sensual reality.

The clearest indication that Plarr's death follows only after a process of resurrection takes place is the fact that he begins to discover within himself the revival of certain feelings of love. As a doctor, he had often touched the pain of the human condition. His response, though, had amounted to only a formal kind of compassion. Nevertheless, he had experienced for some time a vague feeling that such a reaction was deficient, with something of immense significance missing from his life. While hearing people about him constantly invoke love, he has been certain it was a word with a biological explanation, its endurance depending less on its reality than on semantic interest. Because he keeps analyzing the reasons why his life has been without love, however, because, in other words, he keeps fingering the emptiness it has left like a sore, he indicates he really has a longing for the experience of love.

Plarr has an affair with Clara, the young wife of Charley. However, it's merely a sexual arrangement for him at first. Love is based on the qualities of inner peace and innocence, but Plarr is drawn to Clara initially because of a strange form of self-disgust. He falls obsessively for her not out of a sense of physical desire or sexual competition but because she represents a kind of "looking glass" (*HC,* p. 235). What he sees in her is a person who, like himself, goes through the act of love with clinical efficiency. Since she had been a prostitute, she, too, was a professional whose function was to relieve biological discomfort. Like him, he believes, she is not contaminated by emotion.

But neither he nor Clara is as sterile as Plarr at first imagines. She becomes pregnant with his child, falls in love with him, and finally even engenders a creative form of love within him.

After Plarr learned of Clara's pregnancy, he had considered the child to be merely the result of carelessness on his part. Then he had suggested an abortion because the child meant nothing more than a "useless part of Clara like her appendix, perhaps a diseased appendix which ought to be removed" (*HC,* p. 251). Eventually, he can say to himself: "the poor little bastard, if only I could have made some sort of arrangement for it" (*HC,* p. 251). He had been the coldly rational doctor to whom the child meant just "one more wet piece of flesh like any other torn out of the body with a cord which had to be cut" (*HC,* p. 252). In the end, however, the child becomes a real human being to him, a human being whose line of ancestry could never be severed completely. And because Plarr finally realizes that each human being is tied to his past, he wishes he could leave his child a legacy of what he has learned to desire—the ability "to believe in something" (*HC,* p. 252).

At the end of the novel Clara tells Charley she doubts whether Plarr had really learned to care either for her or the child. Significantly enough, Charley disagrees. Plarr, he thinks, was perhaps "a bit slow"; on the other hand, he adds, "it's not so easy to love . . . we make a lot of mistakes" (*HC,* p. 314). Plarr had indeed mistaken Charley's tenderness for weakness and Clara's passion for abasement, for instance. In the end, though, he gains a true comprehension of love. While he is trapped with the little band of rebels holding Charley captive, he learns to believe not in any religious dogma or political ideology but in the terrible beauty of sacrificial love. His father, Leon, the other rebels, and even Clara and Charley, he finally understands, acquire a consecrated gravity having much less to do with a commitment to abstract causes than a willingness to surrender themselves to the demands of human affection. Thus when he takes the ultimate risk of love and is gunned down while trying to save the survivors of the kidnaping plot, he undergoes a violent yet sacred form of baptism.

As is true of many of Greene's novels, the pattern of Plarr's initiation into the realm of love is best described in terms of a journey. Plarr himself imagines during the course of the story that he has embarked in quest of some bewildering end. While he feels himself entering into a strange new region, he has a momentary vision of the prospect. It was "as though he had taken a boat down one of the small tributaries of the Parana and suddenly found himself in some great delta like that of the Amazon, where all sense of direction can be lost" (*HC*, p. 112). The reason he eventually finds the way to self-discovery is because he has had the courage to risk entering the currents of human passion. This is a conclusion which Greene has come to before in his fiction, but never with such emphasis on its dangerous and seemingly necessary paradoxes.

Although Greene injects some comic factors into *The Honorary Consul,* this story obviously represents a shift away from the world he envisioned in *Travels With My Aunt.* In a way, it even represents a shift *back* toward the darker worlds of *A Burnt-Out Case* and *The Comedians,* where the irrational element serves to free people from the entaglements of their egos. Therefore, it might seem at first that Greene had necessarily found the vitalism of Aunt Augusta something to be dismissed as a failure. This would, however, turn out to be a misconception, mainly because it would have to rest on two wrong assumptions—that Greene might believe in one main means of redemption, and that he would feel the necessity to continue writing about his means with certainty. The fact is that Greene is a very restless kind of writer drawn by the uncertainty and variety of experience. He is not a philosophically inclined writer in search of an intellectual system. This is why, as he continues his thematic pursuits, what often happens to him is that once he crosses into a new area, he undergoes a longing or curiosity to see what is ahead or even what he might have left behind. In other words (to use one of his metaphors), he is like a contemporary refugee constantly yearning to cross or re-cross a border. Because this is a continuous aesthetic compulsion, perhaps one shouldn't try to be much more absolute about his central vision than to say that he has the persistent curiosity to see what is on the other side of a character, a theme, or a moral line.

Up to this point, the most conspicuous line Greene has crossed is the one dividing the Catholic novels from the subsequently much more secular stories. Because this movement has resulted in occasional critical controversy, not to mention confusion, it bears some discussion before moving on to Greene's next novel, where he may be perceived as beginning to cross another significant line.

It's a fact that for many years Greene has been categorized by most critics as a Catholic novelist who happens to choose the contemporary scene as a backdrop for his theological themes.[3] Yet the evidence of his last few novels clearly reveals a vision with a wider application, wide enough to actually suggest that it would perhaps be more proper to assign him a place among the novelists of the great humanistic tradition. Even this placement, however, would raise some questions. In short, the more Greene has written, the harder it has become to place a critical label on him.

Greene himself has on more than one occasion tried to warn his readers against putting him into a preconceived category. He once wrote that he "would claim not to be a writer of Catholic novels, but a writer who in four or five books took characters with Catholic ideas for his material."[4] Theological and ethical considerations obviously inform his art, but Greene insists on keeping the characters who represent the facets of his beliefs free of the dogma of systematic thought.[5] At one point Greene even goes so far as to say that he was "not a religious man, though it interests me."[6] Naturally, if his novels are any indication of the man, such a statement calls for qualification. If we can be certain of anything, it's that Greene is a religious novelist, though in a special sense. He is religious in the sense that he contends with the complexities of life in a way which exhibits both sympathetic humanity and insistent reverence. This attitude can be discerned behind all of his novels up to this point. And it's accurate to say that it still continues to dominate in Greene's next novel, even if the conclusion brings on a feeling marked more by ascending despair than hope.

The Human Factor

When Greene began writing *The Human Factor* (1978), he was consciously returning to a familiar territory, the espionage genre. At the same time, he tried to avoid repeating himself by using a different approach from what he was used to. In such earlier spy novels as *The Confidential Agent, The Ministry of Fear,* and *Our Man In Havana,* Greene had succeeded in presenting strikingly idiosyncratic pictures of the world of espionage by exploiting the paradoxical possibilities of nightmarish or romantic melodrama and parody. For many years, though, Greene nursed the ambition to write a highly realistic spy novel which closely reflected the kind of life he had himself experienced as a member of the British Secret Service during the second world war. In his own words, what he wanted to do was "to write a novel of espionage free from the conventional violence," one which presented the Secret Service "unromantically as a way of life, men going daily to their office to earn their pensions, the background much like that of any other profession—whether the bank clerk or the business director—an undangerous routine, and within each charcter the more important private life."[7] Once *The Human Factor* got under way, however, Greene discovered that the story wouldn't always follow his original plan, and could sometimes appear to assume a kind of life of its own.[8] Thus, despite his expressed intentions, violence crept in, and inevitably so did most of Greene's obsessive concerns and stylistic tendencies.[9] These elements took something away from the impression of documentary authenticity Greene had initially hoped for. Yet it's precisely because Greene felt the need to impose his artistic personality on the material that he managed to raise it far above the ordinary spy story.

The story centers on Maurice Castle, a minor official in the British Secret Service. He is 62 years old, rides a bicycle to the train station from which he commutes to London, has a family, owns a dog, and lives in a modest, mortgaged home in Berkhamsted.[10] It seems that he leads an ordinary, rather dull existence.

Because he also has a record of being scrupulous and punctual in his job, he is perceived to be the least likely suspect when a leak is discovered in his department. However, the fact is that, because of his deep love for his black South African wife and grateful loyalty to a communist friend who had helped save her from political murder in her native country, he has become a double agent. For several years he has been passing information about South Africa on to the Russians. All that time he hasn't even come close to being caught. Then his office partner, Davis, is murdered by the Service because it's decided by a higher official that he must be the leak. This cruel mistake gives Castle an opportunity to free himself from his treacherous activities and to gain some hoped-for peace of mind. All he has to do now is keep quiet, whatever information he might come across. But this proves impossible for Castle. Like most of Greene's protagonists, when certain moral imperatives arise, he is driven into responsible action by torments of personal loyalty, guilt, and love.

Some time after Davis' death, Castle finds out about a plan which would have Britain and some of its western allies aid South Africa in the use of nuclear weapons in the event of a serious black African threat against its apartheid system of government. Castle knows that if he leaks the information, he will certainly be discovered this time. Because he finds the moral issue so urgent, however, he goes ahead anyway. Then, as he expected, he is forced to flee to Moscow. What he hadn't expected was that he would have to leave his family behind with apparently no hope of reunion. Consequently, at the end of the story, he is seen as a lonely victim of his sacrificial love.

Given this ending, *The Human Factor* may be read as the most despairing of all of Greene's novels. In none of his stories does personal salvation come without a great deal of anguish. Still, there is always the distinct feeling left that it was all worth it at the end. In *The Human Factor,* the protagonist's humanity was saved before the story even begins, and what unfolds is largely an account of the mental suffering caused by his decision to choose love of individuals close to him over love of country. In Greene's previous novels, the price paid for difficult moral decisions, though never cheap, is ultimately just. In Castle's case, justice (except in the most shallow, political way) seems to be missing, since his actions inspired by love of other human beings are rewarded by implacable insolation.

Has Greene come to the point where he believes that human love, though it may be its own reward, can't in the end change the fact we are all exiles from one another? It seems so, if one considers not only the desolate condition of Castle when the novel ends but also how, in a centrifugal way, he points to several other characters who in their own fashion likewise embody this theme. There are, for example, Davis, who spent a life of romantic decay and frustration before his murder; Colonel Daintry, who is devoured by enforced, frightened silence and insecurity; and old Mr. Halliday, who holds desperately on to a political dream which is a hopeless illusion. Since the list of such casualties could go on, the story finally leaves a powerful impression that loneliness and emotional entrapment are the normal condition in today's world.

It's an impression which is strengthened even more by the use of a figure who works as an absolute foil to Castle and the other characters suffering from this condition. This is Dr. Percival, the man most responsible for the death of Davis. A perfect egoist, he doesn't mind the idea of human separation. In fact, he evidently thrives on it, as an exchange he has with Daintry reveals. It's an exchange where he tries to explain the appropriateness of his view of the Secret Service to Daintry. As he sees it, the Service works precisely because the members "all live in boxes."[11]   To illustrate what he means, he points out a Ben Nicholson painting to Daintry:

> Take a look at that Nicholson. Such a clever balance. Squares of different color. And yet living so happily together. No clash. The man has a wonderful eye. Change just one of the colors—even the size of the square, and it would be no good at all. . . . There's your Section 6. That's your square from now on. You don't need to worry about the blue and the red. All you have to do is pinpoint our man and then tell me. You've no responsibility for what happens in the blue or red squares. In fact not even in the yellow. You just report. No bad conscience. No guilt (*HF*, p. 52).

Daintry is hardly convinced, telling Percival he fails to "understand" these views and wondering out loud if he is being told that action and consequences can have nothing to do with each other. Percival's answer underscores his perverted vision: "The consquences are decided elsewhere, Daintry. . . . Do just try to understand that picture. Particularly the yellow square. If you could only see it with my eyes, you would sleep well tonight" (*HF*, p. 52). Daintry, like Castle, desperately yearns for peace. But in this world, according to Greene, only such characters as Percival can find it in any absolute way. That's because, having no sense of conscience or human involvement, nothing can disturb them in their moral vacancy.

It's not unusual that, somewhere in the course of a story, Greene's characters may say something which can immediately suggest one or more of the stylistic strategies which are used to emphasize the major theme. In *The Human Factor,* the exchange between Percival and Daintry concerning the Secret Service is the most striking example of this tendency. In two ways, at least, it implies how Greene manages to intensify the sense of human separation through style. One way is clear enough. Percival and Daintry talk, but at cross-purposes, without real communication, as if cut off by walls. They are moral opposites, of course, and therefore naturally clash. Yet even characters who otherwise have much in common experience some similar kinds of ineluctable division in this novel. The other way is more subtle, but just as effective. When Percival talks about his vision of squares and boxes, the imagery brings to mind perfectly the idea of human isolation. What's more, it signals how Greene has constructed his story. To reflect his central concern, Greene has, in effect, consciously broken the novel into chapters of mostly similar length and subdivisions. When analyzed closely, these sections appear to have a self-contained quality, as if they were miniature stories in themselves. This doesn't mean the parts aren't arranged together in a most careful way for appropriate development. Nevertheless, Greene manages to create a feeling through this extra-divisional technique that, like the Ben Nicholson painting, the plot structure depends on a rigid scheme of opposition which, in turn, brings to mind the situation of the participants.

Almost as effective as these two ways of stylistically heightening the major theme are several others found throughout the novel. They include the use of unsettling or deceptive foreshadowing, assorted forms of surprising indirection, compressed symbolism, and unexpected satire or irony. These are elements which may have become an automatic part of Greene's method by now. Still, they are completely appropriate to the subject matter, as are two additional stylistic approaches which Greene uses with greater self-consciousness. The first of these is the use of a combination of a flattened, unadorned language and a quiet, almost weary tone. It's a combination certainly fitting for a story about desolation. The second has to do with the way the description details are presented. Especially when filtered through Castle, these details appear neurotically precise and factual, with a peculiar amount of attention paid to the most minor items.[12] This approach, too, is fitting, for it helps one to better comprehend a character who perceives things like a foreigner or exile among strangers.

As a result of the various successful methods used by Greene in presenting a picture of desolation, one has to look hard for any signs of hope or affirmation. They exist, nevertheless, and can be discovered through inferential or reverse analysis of the loneliest, apparently most ineffectual characters. In their failures, these characters seem to carry despair around like an infection. In Greene's world, however, failure is never quite what it seems. Often, in fact, it's the paradoxical indication of essential humanity. This is precisely the case with such characters as Davis, Daintry, old Mr. Halliday and, most notably, Castle. That's why, in dwelling on Castle's fate, it would be wrong to merely pity him. In the final analysis, he has something which is to be profoundly desired. If he becomes a victim of the unfairness of life, it's because he believes in the importance of the human heart. He is convinced that love is an enormous risk which must be taken, whatever the cost.

Castle also thinks that "a man in love walks through the world like an anarchist, carrying a time bomb" (*HF*, p. 185). Greene makes it clear this is one kind of anarchy which would be a blessing. What would be endangered would be the perversions of the contemporary political world. If love really were let loose, the cynical ways of the world powers, nurtured by the perpetuation of blind patriotism, couldn't survive. Then, a higher loyalty would take over—to one's family and friends—and Castle's kind of disloyalty would appear as virtue.

Such an ideal time may never arrive, of course, since there are too many modern barbarians like Percival around. These people value only one thing, and it has nothing to do with caring for other people or their beliefs. All Percival wants, he says, is "to be on the side most likely to win" and to "enjoy the game we're all playing" (*HF*, p. 215). If he fears anything, it's people who believe in something besides power, because this makes them uncontrollable. He goes, therefore, to any lengths to defeat them. At the end of *The Human Factor*, it seems he has won "the game." However, the moral scheme and principles which course through the novel point to another conclusion. Those characters who can sacrifice themselves for their fellow man may lose a great deal in the process, but they save their humanity. Those who don't have this "human factor" are lost, and whatever other advantages they may hold, lead the most dispossessed lives of all.

In establishing this thematic line, Greene has exhibited nearly perfect control of his writing skills. On a couple of occasions the logical structure of the plot strains a bit, and Greene's evocative allusions to several famous literary works may strike one as overly insistent. But these flawas can't be cited as doing any real harm to the story's impact; and if there are any other technical imperfections, they are even more minor. The reviews which met *The Human Factor*, recognizing all this, were by and large very favorable. What few critical notices there were objected to what was perceived to be Greene's diminished moral vision.

Representative of this fundamental objection is the critic who, after asserting that *The Human Factor* turns on the issue of apartheid, makes the following conclusion:

> The simplest thing to say about *The Human Factor* is that it fails as fiction because the characters are all puppets. . . . The reason the characters are lifeless and the action contrived is that Greene has narrowed the scope of his artistic vision. In the Catholic world the struggle is over human souls, and no earthly gain is worth the loss of a single one of them. Christians know this; atheists and others can comprehend the conflict, the terms of which do not change from century to century. The center remains constant, whatever alteration fashion and superficial detail may undergo. But . . . the artist must transcend the specific uses of history and politics because they are relative at best and always ephemeral, and the artist's concern is not with what is transitory, but with that which endures.[13]

How seriously can one take these views? Upon consideration, not seriously at all. There is a misunderstanding, to begin with, that apartheid is the main theme. Yet, granted that the subject of apartheid acts as an essential catalyst in the story, it's "apartness" in the largest, human sense which becomes the real issue. From this misunderstanding follow the other conclusions which are equally misguided because they don't really spring from the novel itself. Instead, they turn out to be views imposed on the novel because of a pre-disposition typical, incidentally, of all those critics who have had trouble adjusting to Greene's shifts in perspective ever since he turned more secular after his Catholic novels. In actual fact, after the Catholic novels, Greene has continued to write just as much about "that which endures." Depending on the novel, one may call Greene's enduring subjects man's soul or man's heart, or the politics of eschatology or the human factor. Whatever the reference, in the final analysis, it's clear these are aspects of fundamentally the same, on-going moral concerns. In *The Human Factor,* this attitude is obviously still driving the artistic vision. Only now, apparently more pessimistic about contemporary life than ever, Greene has narrowed the means of personal salvation to an extreme.

Doctor Fischer of Geneva, or the Bomb Party

The sense of despair found in *The Human Factor* is, if anything, even more profound in Greene's subsequent book of fiction. *Doctor Fischer of Geneva, or the Bomb Party* (1980), a novella rather than a full-fledged novel, is told by a protagonist whose story sounds even sadder than that of Castle. His name is Alfred Jones, and as he tells it, his life has been a process of losing. An Englishman, he has retreated to a job as a translator for a chocolate factory in Switzerland. In settling in this neutral country, he left behind a past which saw him lose his wife, his parents, one of his hands, and, apparently, all hope of happiness. Then, by what seems like a miracle, he meets a beautiful young woman who responds to the love he begins to feel for her. This is the daughter of Doctor Fischer, a cynical millionaire known for the cavity-fighting toothpaste he invented and the notorious parties he throws for some of his rich, greedy acquaintances. When the lovers decide to marry, Jones feels obligated to inform the father. Doctor Fischer, however, could care less, being much more interested in how Jones, a poor man, might behave at one of his parties for the wealthy.

When Jones finally goes to one of these parties, he discovers that the host is apparently just as cruel or mad as his reputation has him. At the party, Doctor Fischer makes his guests undergo debasement before they can claim the expensive presents which, despite their own wealth, they are desperate to have. Jones is so offended by this ritual of humiliation he decides never to attend another such party. Then his young wife dies in a skiing accident, and Jones, in a self-destructive frame of mind, decides to accept Doctor Fischer's invitation to attend his last party. At that party, after driving his guests to the limits of humiliating greed, Doctor Fischer commits suicide. And Jones, who has wished and tried to kill himself following the death of his second wife, is left behind, now without even the belief that death, much less life, could make sense.

What is the point of such a story besides the fact that Jones' absurdly painful situation calls for our sympathy? That's not an easy question to answer because of the cunning way this book is written. At first glance, it may seem to be told in the most straightforward, simple language whose function is to be as clear as possible. Then it becomes increasingly obvious that all the important details of dialogue and description are used in such a way as to resonate with dense, compound meaning. In addition, it's only a surface impression that the story's structure consists simply of a chronological flashback framed by a kind of prologue and epilogue. Greene also employs some structural (as well as stylistic) elements of allegory, fable, fairy tale, and detective story. Finally, the story is told in a tone which can only be called gay despair, a combination prone to leave the reader suspended somewhere between laughter and tears.

Greene manages to exploit this remarkable mixture of style, structure, and tone in such a way the story promises, in a tantalizing fashion, that there are various possible ways to read it. Thus *Doctor Fischer of Geneva* may be read, for example, as a confessional about betrayal; a parabolic study of the nature of evil; a dialectic on the distinction between hating and despising; a commentary on the sickness of greed; an existential love story; or even as an ironic presentation of the strengths and weaknesses of a novelist's self-created world and mind.[14] It may also be interpreted as Greene's most pessimistic word on his life-long pursuit of salvation.

For such a reading, one must be guided by the story's allegorical aspects. Through the book, there are imposing suggestions that we are to imagine things, even if ironically, both in a realistic and religious perspective. Certainly this is true of the settings Greene chooses and the action he invents. Thus, for example, Doctor Fischer holds his last party in his snow-covered garden (antithetically edenic) and serves his guests with a final banquet (or last supper) before he offers them (communion-like) Christmas crackers, all but one containing two million franc checks and the last one supposedly a bomb (or the final risk of punishment).

This double perspective is also applied to the characters. Alfred Jones, as his name implies, is an ordinary man (Jones) who is partly held by a past faith or tradition (he was almost christened Aelfred). The guests who attend the parties are referred to as "Toads" since they (piously) toady up to a host who dispenses presents and humiliation. Doctor Fischer's daughter is angelic and, despite her gender, even remindful of Christ in her purity. As for Doctor Fischer, he is set up to make us think of God. But if he is God-like, it's in a cruel and fallacious way (he is not a real doctor), for his ambition is to ensnare (to fish for) his victims. In other words, he has elements of both Jehovah and Satan and none of Christ.

By injecting Doctor Fischer with so much religious significance, Greene manages to use him in two important ways. Through his words and actions, Doctor Fischer becomes an abrasive foil to Jones. This allows us to understand Jones' situation more clearly. Even more important, Doctor Fischer is used as an oblique or metaphorical reflection of Greene's beliefs. This is why, by considering Doctor Fischer carefully, one can come to a true understanding of Greene's final moral vision.

Greene has evidently reached the point where he imagines (and *only* imagines) a God who must have some of Doctor Fischer's worst features. One of these is greed, a form of greed which is, however, quite distinct from the kind the "Toads" exhibit. In one of the key exchanges in the book, Doctor Fischer indicates just what kind of greed he feels. In response to Jones' question as to whether or not there are limits to his greed, Doctor Fischer says: "Perhaps I shall find out one day. But my greed is of a different kind. . . . I like to think that my greed is a little more like God's." Pressed to explain himself, Doctor Fischer launches into a discussion which, one is indirectly led to believe, actually represents one of Greene's personal speculations:

> Well, the believers and the sentimentalists say that he [God] is greedy for our love. I prefer to think that, judging from the world he is supposed to have made, he can only be greedy for our humiliation, and *that* greed how could he ever exhaust? It's bottomless. The world grows more and more miserable while he twists the endless screw, though he gives us presents—for a universal suicide would defeat his purpose—to alleviate the humilia-

tions we suffer. A cancer of the rectum, a streaming
cold, incontinence. For example, you are a poor man, so
he gives you a small present, my daughter, to keep you
satisfied a little longer.

Jones wonders out loud why God would wish to humiliate the
human race. Doctor Fischer's significant response is as follows:

Don't I wish to humiliate? And they say he made us in
his image. Perhaps he found he was a rather bad crafts-
man and he is disappointed in the result. One throws a
faulty article into the dustbin.[15]

In all of Greene there is no repartee which is darker in its implications about man's fate. From all indications, Greene now believes, there couldn't be a God. But even if there were, one
could certainly not love Him. How could one love a power
which, as represented by Doctor Fischer, would seem to make
all human beings undergo humiliating suffering because they are
faulty creations in the first place. One could only despise such a
God.

Much of this story turns on the difference between despising and hating. Once again, it's Doctor Fischer's words which,
when they are placed in a thematic perspective, seem to summarize Greene's own thoughts on the matter. To Jones' statement
that there was no one he despises more, Doctor Fischer says:

Again you are using the wrong term. Semantics are
important, Jones. I tell you, you hate, you don't despise.
To despise comes out of a great disappointment. Most
people are not capable of a great disappointment, and I
doubt if you are. Their expectations are too low for that.
When one despises, Jones, it's like a deep and incurable
wound, the beginning of death. And one must revenge
one's wound while there's still time. When the one who
inflicted it is dead, one has to strike back at others (*DF,*
pp. 116-117).

Doctor Fischer recognizes this emotion as a sickness. Yet once
he has caught it, he consciously nurtures it to combat the possibility of hurt pride. What he doesn't forsee is that this is such a
contagious emotion it may spread to cover the whole world,

including perhaps finally oneself.

This is, indeed, what happens to Doctor Fischer. He comes to despise himself, and he kills himself. The question then has to arise: what can this mean in the allegorical sense? The answer seems to point directly at what has happened to Greene's religious faith. God no longer exists, because, for Greene, he has committed suicide. To put it in a less exotic way, the idea of God has died in his mind. In looking at the body of Doctor Fischer, Jones thinks that it contained "no more significance than a dead dog" (*DF,* p. 153). Now this antagonist whom he had sometimes compared to Jehovah and Satan was just a "bit of rubbish" (*DF,* p. 153). Jones (with whom Greene finally identifies) now knows that, although good and evil obviously exist, there is no supernatural mystery behind them. At the heart of existence is a void, and only a personal vision can give life moral substance or meaning.

Greene still is interested in the *idea* of God. But he realizes it's just a mental construct or dream, and in *Doctor Fischer of Geneva* he more emphatically than ever before expresses this conclusion. Typically, Greene often couches his most serious considerations in paradox. That's why it comes as no surprise that in this book his main spokesman turns out to be, in an ironic and inverted way, the villainous Doctor Fischer. Jones, however, is allowed to express some of Greene's conclusions, too. In fact, it's a dream of his which, by itself, perhaps best summarizes Greene's ultimate vision:

> I fell asleep as I had the day before, suddenly, in my chair, and I saw Doctor Fischer with his face painted like a clown's and his mustache trained upward like the Kaiser's as he juggled with eggs, never breaking one. He drew fresh ones from his elbow, from his arse, from the air—he created eggs, and at the end there must have been hundreds in the air. His hands moved around them like birds and then he clapped his hands and they fell to the ground and exploded and I woke (*DF,* p. 121).

Like his protagonist, Greene has held on to "at least a half-belief" in God (*DF,* p. 143). Finally, though, he can only imagine a universe which, at best, is run by a clown who carelessly juggles with our lives. And if there is no such clown, precisely, what Greene has awakened to is the full conviction we are all trapped in a black comedy from which we can only be temporarily saved by means of individual love and, to some extent, an absurdist's sense of indomitable humor.

Monsignor Quixote

In *Monsignor Quixote* (1982), his most recently published story, Greene doesn't break any crucial new ground. Nevertheless, this short novel could hardly be ignored in a survey of Greene's major fiction. Because Greene manages to express his personally developed morality with so much natural facility and genuine feeling, it is possible to look on the story as his most forthright word on the subject of human redemption.

The stylistic method Greene uses in *Monsignor Quixote* to present his latest thoughts on this subject consists of a mixture of most of his characteristic strategies. Yet two of these do bear special notice, not only because Greene employs them so prominently but also because they serve as natural exponents of the kind of story we have. These two strategies may be referred to as paradoxical juxtaposition (allied with parody) and rhetorical drama (allied with philosophical debate).

As the title suggests, *Monsignor Quixote* is a venerative parody of Cervantes' great story. Of course, Greene only draws upon Cervantes in order to fit the material to his own distinctly imagined, ironically compared world. Thus in his tale the central character is also an unlikely picaresque hero who champions dreams. This Quixote, however, is one of Greene's recognizable characters, a humble village priest whose books of chivalry are represented by religious volumes. Like his literary ancestor, he has a Sancho. Only this one happens to be a Communist who once studied for the priesthood before going into local politics and finally becoming the mayor of the village. It's an odd pair, but that's precisely why they are thrown together by the destiny Greene invents for them. What brings them together as traveling companions is the misfortune of sudden displacement. The priest is unexpectedly promoted to Monsignor and the politician is thrown out of office by a swing to the right in local elections. Thus they decide to escape by taking a vacation in Rocinante, Monsignor Quixote's beloved old car. On the road, they will meet many adventures. Most will turn out to be wildly comical, but others will carry danger with them. The last adventure, in fact, will lead to Monsignor Quixote's premature death.

In Greene's fiction the value of a protagonist's death always has to be questioned, and our response is bound to be made up of opposing feelings. Thus the death of Monsignor Quixote, one of Greene's most engaging and wise characters, makes us feel a despairing sadness or even bitterness. At the same time, a different, quite hopeful feeling sets in. We begin to realize that the entire story doesn't end there, since Greene manages to indicate that his protagonist has left a permanent, affirmative effect behind.

In partial preparation for such a conclusion, Greene sets up a series of contrasts which the story compels us to resolve. For example, he juxtaposes the Gospel with the Communist Manifesto, Torquemada with Stalin, the Roman Curia with the Politbureau, and the Opus Dei with the Guardia Civil of Spain. Each time, an inherent lesson becomes clear. The lines between various beliefs and their excrescences, and finally even between fact and fiction, are very fine, if they exist at all. This realization—that truth is ambiguous and depends on an appreciation of paradox—leads to wisdom. Just one more thing need be added. True wisdom, having more to do with doubt than certainty, has as its primary reward the knowledge of the greatest mystery, creative human love.

Without being fully aware of it, Monsignor Quixote is the wisest man in the story. At first his traveling companion doesn't seem to realize this fact, either. By the time Monsignor Quixote dies, though, the ex-mayor comes to a real appreciation of what his friend has taught him. The story can therefore be seen as representing the proper education of a man with a limited understanding of the world, which is to say a political one. Yet in the final analysis, the ex-mayor isn't put into the story simply as a kind of vessel for received wisdom. Because of his inquiring and sympathetic mind, he serves both to inspire the best feelings and thoughts in Monsignor Quixote and to reflect the continuously questioning side of Greene's mind.

The questioning tendency of Greene's mind is reflected more directly in *Monsignor Quixote* than in any of his previous novels due to the story's design. It's framed primarily as a kind of rhetorical drama consisting of a series of speculative debates. On the most obvious level, these debates are taking place between the major characters of this voluble story. Yet they may concurrently be read as the sorts of mental dialogues Greene has been having with himself all his life. Greene must have been aware that such a self-consciously rhetorical approach had its built-in risk. The story could easily have sunk into confessional, forced didacticism. To avoid this trap, Greene makes every effort to see that his debaters philosophize those thoughts which would naturally arise from their personalities and experiences. This is why we can believe in the redemptive ending of the story. Greene may have had his intentions clear in his mind all along; but when we reach the final scene where the ex-mayor is made to fulfill the story's promise, the feeling of spontaneous inevitability is there mainly because of the credible and unaffected way human nature has been pictured.

After the death of Monsignor Quixote, the ex-mayor has just the sort of experience which may save humanity. During their travels, he had learned a great deal about the ambiguities and paradoxes of life. Of this he was consciously aware. What he was not fully aware of was that he had also been prepared all along to enter the profoundest, most permanent mysteries of human existence. In the final lines of the story, he wonders: "Why is it that the hate of a man—even of a man like Franco—dies with his death, and yet love, the love which he had begun to feel for Father Quixote, seemed now to live and grow in spite of the final separation and the final silence—for how long, he wondered with a kind of fear, was it possible for that love of his to continue? And to what end?"[16] The answers to these questions have been taught, at least indirectly, by the example and pronouncements of Monsignor Quixote. Clearly, they are the same ones which Greene has offered in his previous books. Personal love is fearful in its power. It's so powerful that it can even make us leap into realms of faith where love becomes a transcendent force.

The seriousness with which Greene looks on this issue may be measured, ironically, by the one obvious stylistic flaw in an otherwise extremely polished work. Greene's presentation becomes a bit heavy-handed at the point where his protagonist is faced with the cynical corruption of his beliefs. Monsignor Quixote has come upon a procession of the Virgin Mary, and what he sees shocks him:

> It was impossible to see the robes for all the paper money —hundred-peseta notes, thousand-peseta notes, a five-

hundred-franc note, and right over the heart a hundred-dollar bill. Between him and the statue there were only the priest and the fumes of the incense from his censer. Father Quixote gazed up at the crowned head and the glassy eyes which were like those of a woman dead and neglected—no one bothered even to lower her lids. He thought: Was it for this she saw her son die in agony? To collect money? To make a priest rich (*MQ,* p. 198)?

To this rather bluntly represented blasphemy, Monsignor Quixote must react with indignation. Yet it seems somewhat out of character for him to go so far as to first try to block the procession physically, and then, having gone on to act with the kind of aggression more to be expected of a street insurgent, to declare that one "can't start a revolution without bloodshed" (*MQ,* p. 101). It's a startling conclusion on the part of Monsignor Quixote, and doesn't seem to come naturally enough from him. Then how is one to explain its presence? The apparent answer underscores an aspect of Greene which must ultimately be emphasized. There is still the wide-spread perception that Greene has always been primarily concerned with telling an entertaining story.[17] But the aforementioned episode, and the peculiar way in which it is flawed, allows us to have at least a glimpse of another, more important, ambition. From the beginning, Greene has been intent on using his talents to present his moral vision, sometimes with so much intensity, in fact, that his aesthetic conception may be overwhelmed by the depth of his feelings. In other words, Greene feels so strongly about some things that he is inclined to present them very directly. At no time is this urge more evident than when he confronts willful depravity, especially the cheapening of the human soul.

VII.
A LOOK AT THE FINAL ACHIEVEMENT

Although Greene has long ago reached an age when one would expect him to consider retirement, he has indicated that his urge to write continues unabated.[1] Therefore, it's possible *Monsignor Quixote* may not turn out to be his last book of fiction. But even if Greene manages to keep on publishing, it now seems possible to outline his achievement as a novelist without the danger of the sorts of premature summations which so many of his earlier critics have run up against. With the appearance of *Monsignor Quixote* it seems that his greatest thematic subject has now been fully imparted, or has at least reached a resolute, inescapably abstract conclusion which in future novels could only be repeated, whatever different stylistic forms might be tried.

In summarizing Greene's accomplishments, it's useful to begin with the question of his contemporary reputation. Among most critics, not to mention the general reading public, it's indeed very high. Yet Greene also has his share of detractors, especially in some academic circles. This is all to the good when these critics point out the flaws which can be found in Greene's various efforts. Certain of these same critics, however, go much further, concluding that Greene shouldn't even be considered as a major novelist. What is. the basis for such a conclusion? Almost without exception, these critics feel that Greene, even if he possesses great natural talents, falls through in two important ways. One, he isn't consistent enough in his moral vision and, two, he isn't an entirely original writer. Obviously, if true, these would be legitimate reasons for attacking Greene's reputation. However, the first of these objections can be dismissed immediately by recalling how the theme of salvation ties all of his novels together. As for the second objection, it seems to have basis in fact only if one is arguing from a modernist bias.

If one is to judge Greene's achievement properly, it should be recognized that he *consciously* has tried to write a new kind of novel which at the same time is traditional. To see this, one has to first imagine Greene as a beginning novelist standing at a crossroad, pulled in two different directions. On the one hand, there was the traditional side. Here would lie the typical British novel in which character, story, and moral theme were the primary virtues. Here would be found the socially realistic fiction which, it may be argued, began with Chaucer and has continued through such writers as Fielding, Thackeray, Dickens, and Hardy. On the other hand, there was the modernist possibility. This possibility—with its emphasis on experimental technique as a means of primarily expressing not social issues but the resonant contingencies of an isolated artistic sensibility and medium—actually held most of Greene's interest during the first part of his career. Feeling the great influence of James Joyce and other experimentalists writing at that time, Greene injected his earliest novels with a highly poetic, purposely devised language. These novels were failures, and Greene, recognizing that the modernist way was actually alien to him, turned for guidance toward such writers as Henry James and Joseph Conrad. In other words, he opted for an older, pre-modernist heritage. To a number of his critics, this apparently seemed simply a retreat to a safer, more popular way. Greene's writings, once he took this step, did become increasingly popular. This happened, however, not because Greene played it safe, but because he then began to risk injecting an old tradition with thoroughly contemporary ideas and patterns. Subsequently, he became so adept at this process that, in effect, he would up re-creating the realist novel for our times.

In producing such a novel, Greene has combined four essential facets. To begin with, he has re-emphasized narrative, functional style, and other artistic virtues closely associated with the realist tradition. He has also cultivated the possibilities of various popular genres and themes and employed them for dramatic effect. Then, through the main force of a moral vision, he has raised his novels to psychological and symbolic levels which are characteristic of the most serious kind of art. Finally, by focusing directly on contemporary issues with a vivid religious and political imagination, Greene has shown how pertinent and alive the realist novel can still be.

At this juncture a question concerning Greene's influence might be raised. If one claims that he has rejuvenated the traditional novel, does this mean he actually has followers? The answer is, only indirectly. This was bound to be so since Greene is such a highly obsessive and privately romantic writer. With regard to his artistic vision, it seems that he is wholly unique. Yet, in looking especially at the literary scene in England, it's possible to see a definite measure of his influence. For a long time after the modernist revolution, it was difficult to find a serious realist writer in England. Without getting into a debate as to the comparative merits of these opposing literary fashions, it's clear that for historical and ideological reasons, the realist rather than the modernist novel seems more natural to the British writer as a whole. But it's only after Greene came into his own and provided (along to an important extent with Evelyn Waugh) an influential example that the realist novel made a sort of comeback in England. Today, the modernist tradition seems still to be the most influential one in France and America, for example. In England, however, only a handful of writers still appears to subscribe to its tenets. There it's essential traditionalists who are now in the forefront of critical acclaim.[2] The likely indications are that all these writers were touched by the long shadow of Greene, and, not to make exaggerated claims, were at least encouraged to try his direction.

In summarizing Greene's achievement, though, what should be stressed above everything else is something which he has in common with all major writers of whatever tradition. That is that Greene has managed to create an imagined world which is immediately recognizable as his alone. What's under consideration here isn't mainly the characters and placement of his stories, although they are strikingly unique. More important is Greene's moral system. This is where Greene is finally most creative. Feeling the powerful need for a moral system, but ultimately finding none which he could unquestionably adopt, he has done what other great novelists before him were compelled to do.[3] In effect, he has invented a personal moral system which gives integrity and completeness to his whole fictional world. At the heart of this system lies the conviction that we must all be driven by inner pursuits of our salvation.

October 2, 1904 Born at Berkhamsted, Hertfordshire
1925   *Babbling April* (poetry)
1929   *The Man Within*
1932   *Stamboul Train (Orient Express)*
1934   *It's a Battlefield*
1935   *England Made Me (The Shipwrecked)*
1936   *Journey Without Maps* (travel)
                 A Gun for Sale (This Gun for Hire)
1938   *Brighton Rock*
1939   *The Lawless Roads (Another Mexico)* (travel)
                 The Confidential Agent
1940   *The Power and the Glory*
1943   *The Ministry of Fear*
1947   *Nineteen Stories* (short stories)
1948   *The Heart of the Matter*
1950   *The Third Man* (screenplay design)
1951   *The Lost Childhood* (essays)
                 The End of the Affair
1953   *The Living Room* (play)
                 Essays catholiques (essays)
1954   *Twenty-One Stories* (short stories)
1955   *Loser Takes All* (novella)
                 The Quiet American
1957   *The Potting Shed* (play)
1958   *Our Man in Havana*
1959   *The Complaisant Lover* (play)
1961   *In Search of a Character* (travel)
                 A Burnt-Out Case
1963   *A Sense of Reality* (short stories)
1964   *Carving a Statue* (play)
1966   *The Comedians*
1967   *May We Borrow Your Husband?* (short stories)
1969   *Collected Essays* (essays)

1969	*Travels with My Aunt*
1971	*A Sort of Life* (autobiography)
1973	*The Honorary Consul*
1974	*Lord Rochester's Monkey* (biography)
1975	*The Return of A. J. Raffles* (play)
1978	*The Human Factor*
1980	*The Pleasure Dome* (film criticism)
	Doctor Fischer of Geneve, or the Bomb Party (novella)
	Ways of Escape (autobiography)
1982	*Monsignor Quixote*

IX.
FOOTNOTES

I. A Different Approach

[1] One of the latest studies on Greene, as a matter of fact, is organized around this issue. Peter Wolfe, *Graham Greene the Entertainer* (Carbondale, Illinois: Southern Illinois University Press, 1972).

[2] The most obvious example of this kind of approach is the book by John Atkins. John Atkins, *Graham Greene: A Biographical and Literary Study* (London: J. Calder, 1957).

[3] The Catholic critics have been particularly eager to try a label on Greene. This desire has led some of them into critical acrobatics. F. L. Kunkel, for example, in his attempt to describe Greene's beliefs precisely, falls into a sophistic trap by finally calling Greene a half-Manichean. See Francis L. Kunkel, *The Labyrinthine Ways of Graham Greene* (New York: Sheed & Ward, 1960). Reissued in 1973 by Paul P. Appel, Mamaroneck, New York.

[4] The most obvious example is the book by Allott and Farris. Kenneth Allot and Miriam Farris, *The Art of Graham Greene* (London: Hamish Hamilton, 1951).

[5] V. S. Pritchett, "The Human Factor in Graham Greene," *The New York Times Magazine* (February 26, 1978), p. 40.

II. Finding His Way

[1] As well as on the art of film, one might add. See his book, *The Pleasure Dome* (London: Secker & Warburg, 1972).

[2] See his essays on Henry James in *Collected Essays* (New York: The Viking Press, 1969), pp. 23-53.

[3] The most important sources for this kind of commentary are his autobiographical works *A Sort of Life* (New York: Simon and Schuster, 1971) and *Ways of Escape* (New York: Simon and Schuster, 1980). In addition, there is his very revealing essay "The Revolver in the Corner

Cupboard" in *The Lost Childhood* (New York: The Viking Press, 1951).

[4]*A Sort of Life*, pp. 117-118.

[5]*Journey Without Maps* (New York: The Viking Press, 1965), pp. 220-221.

[6]*Another Mexico* (New York: The Viking Press, 1967), p. 2. Known primarily as *The Lawless Roads* in England.

[7]*Ibid.*, pp. 2-3.

[8]*Collected Essays*, p. 17.

[9]*Ibid.*, pp. 18-19.

[10]*Ibid.*, p. 18.

[11]This was not Greene's first time to flirt with suicide. Some five or six years earlier he had, on various occasions, tried hypo, hayfever lotion, nightshade, and twenty aspirins before taking a swim as means of suicide. Then he was driven primarily by a romantic sense of rebellion.

[12]Greene took this trip during the winter of 1934-35. One year later he published his observations in his *Journey Without Maps*, quite a unique travel book which reveals much more about the traveler than about the land.

[13]*Journey Without Maps*, pp. 262, 279.

[14]Kenneth Allott and Miriam Farris, *The Art of Graham Greene* (New York: Russell & Russell, Inc., 1963), p. 15.

[15]*A Sort of Life*, p. 196.

[16]It was, for example, praised for its "brisk" and "exceptionally fresh and readable story" of "vitally delineated" characters (Thomas Gilbert, "First Novels," *Spectator*, June 22, 1929, p. 982); for its "honesty and subtlety" (Bartlet Brebner, *The Saturday Review of Literature*, October 19, 1929, p. 287); and for the "skill and complexity with which the psychological tissue is woven" (Anonymous, *The Times Literary Supplement*, June 20, 1929, p. 492).

[17]Also known as *Orient Express* in the United States.

[18]The most noteworthy of which is Quin Savory, the popular writer. On one hand, he is satirized for writing trash. On the other, he is a kind of sly parody of Greene himself. Greene, as fond of self-deprecating humor as anyone, attributes certain qualities to him which he recognizes in himself. For example, he makes Savory out to be a kind of "spy" who has learned some of his craft from films and who feels that the world is an "adventurous place."

[19]*A Sort of Life*, p. 203.

[20]This is apparently one reason why Greene decided to make up the label of "entertainment" for it.

[21]Interestingly enough, part of the original inspiration for this book was a famous film, *Grand Hotel.* But in its make-up, it resembles much

more the work in the *film noir* genre of Fritz Lang, a director whose films Greene admired.

[22] Greene believes that this practice was due to "the influence of my early passion for playwrighting," a passion "which has never died" and which eventually led to several plays. *Ways of Escape,* p. 32.

[23] *Stamboul Train* (London: William Heinemann & Bodley Head, 1974), p. 203.

[24] In certain ways, Czinner is a type of figure which continued to fascinate Greene and which he eventually split into two characters, the whiskey priest and the lieutenant in *The Power and the Glory.*

[25] Another modern novelist who used authorial comments was Francois Mauriac, a writer whom Greene admired and who apparently influenced him.

[26] David Lodge, "Graham Greene," *Six Contemporary British Novelists,* George Stade, ed. (New York: Columbia University Press, 1976), p. 24.

[27] Greene's recollection that the novel's subject "was suggested by a dream, the fruit of anxiety-ridden weeks, in which I had been condemned to death for murder" and that as he wrote it he felt he was going through "an act of self-destruction" may help to explain the book's unrelieved gloom. *Ways of Escape,* pp. 34-35.

[28] Also known as *The Shipwrecked* in the United States.

[29] Greene says that the rise of Hitler was one of the factors that "cast a shadow on this book." *Ways of Escape,* p. 37.

[30] *England Made Me* (London: William Heinemann & Bodley Head, 1970), p. 256.

[31] Even though, as he recalls, this is "the only occasion when I have deliberately chosen an unknown country as a background and then visited it, like a camera team, to take the necessary stills." *Ways of Escape,* p. 37.

[32] He managed this in part by the use of suggestive cataloguing, a practice which he may have learned from Auden and his followers.

[33] This is true despite Greene's belief that the brother and sister are two of his very best portraits. *Ways of Escape,* pp. 39-40.

[34] Also known as *This Gun for Hire* in the United States.

[35] In *Ways of Escape* Greene says that in looking back to the two books "Raven the killer seems to me now a first sketch for Pinkie in *Brighton Rock,*" p. 75.

III. The Catholic Novels

[1] This initial inconclusiveness was reflected by the fact that when the

book first appeared it was listed as a novel, then an entertainment, then back to a novel in Greene's bibliography.

[2] *Ways of Escape,* pp. 78-79.

[3] In *Ways of Escape,* Greene admits that this is so and wishes that he had the "strength of mind" to "start the story again," p. 80.

[4] Interview with Gene D. Phillips, "Graham Greene: On the Screen," *Graham Greene,* Samuel Hynes, ed. (Englewood Cliffs, Prentice-Hall, Inc., 1973), p. 173.

[5] Evelyn Waugh, "Felix Culpa?" *Graham Greene,* Samuel Hynes, ed. (Englewood Cliffs: Prentice-Hall, Inc., 1973), p. 96.

[6] R. W. B. Lewis, "The 'Trilogy'," *The Power and the Glory,* R. W. B. Lewis and Peter J. Conn, eds. (New York: The Viking Press, 1970), p. 377.

[7] Frederick R. Karl, *The Contemporary English Novel* (New York: Farrar, Straus and Giroux, 1965), p. 93. Even Charles A. Muller, who has written convincingly about Greene's recent novels, holds this view: "Graham Greene and the Justification of God's Ways," *UES* 10,i (1972), pp. 23-35.

[8] Robert O. Evans, "The Satanist Fallacy of *Brighton Rock,*" *Graham Greene,* Robert O. Evans, ed. (University of Kentucky Press, 1963), p. 154.

[9] Graham Greene, *Brighton Rock* (London: William Heinemann & Bodley Head, 1975), p. 120. All further references to this book will be incorporated into the body of the text, with abbreviations for the title *BR* followed by page numbers both within parentheses, a system which will be used with subsequent novels by Greene.

[10] This is at least partly explained by an admission Greene made in his second autobiographical work: "I fell back for the first and last time in my life on Benzedrine. For six weeks I started each day with a tablet, and renewed the dose at midday. Each day I sat down to work with no idea of what turn the plot might take and each morning I wrote, with the automatism of a planchette, two thousand words instead of my usual stint of five hundred words." *Ways of Escape,* p. 92.

[11] *The Confidential Agent* (London: William Heinemann & Bodley Head, 1971), p. 167.

[12] Also known as *Another Mexico,* in the United States primarily.

[13] *Ways of Escape,* p. 86.

[14] Kunkel has pointed out a number of parallels between the two: the priest is betrayed by a Judas figure, spends a night in a cell that is remindful of Gethsemane, is tempted by worldliness in the desert-like land across the border, gives solace to a "good thief" in the person of the Yank, is more the target of the state than the Barabas-like criminal, is denied by a fallen disciple of the church as his death approaches, and finally dies a martyr

for the corrupt and abandoned. Francis L. Kunkel, *The Labyrinthine Ways of Graham Greene* (New York: Sheed and Ward, 1959), p. 118.

[15]Lynette Kohn, *Graham Greene: The Major Novels* (Palo Alto: Stanford Honors Essays in Humanities, no. IV, 1961), pp. 41-43. Or, if one wishes, circles of another kind. Patten thinks that there is a "radiant" pattern, with the priest "at the center, and all of the others characters . . . symbolically related to him, as the spokes of a wheel relate to the hub." Karl Patten, "The Structure of *The Power and the Glory*," *The Power and the Glory*, R. W. B. Lewis and Peter Conn, eds. (New York: The Viking Press, 1970), p. 311.

[16]Karl goes too far, though, when he says that "Greene's mission in his major novels . . . is to write Greek tragedy without forsaking a Christian God." Karl, p. 88. More credible is Patten's suggestion that in the figure of the priest we have both "the type of Everyman, that primitive product of the late medieval imagination" and someone who resembles Bunyan's Christian. Patten, p. 321.

[17]Graham Greene, *The Power and the Glory* (New York: The Viking Press, 1948), p. 45.

[18]Atkins' argument that the priest was able to go on because he was sustained less by faith than by force of habit and "nihilism of the opposition" is a rather cynical one based less on textual evidence than, one must assume, on personal bias. John Atkins, *Graham Greene* (London: J. Calder, 1957), p. 124.

[19]The fact that Greene chose to call it an "entertainment" signals, though it doesn't explain, this fact.

[20]*Nineteen Stories* (London: Heinemann, 1947).

[21]Graham Greene, *The Ministry of Fear* (London: William Heinemann, 1956), p. 71.

[22]Several critics have discovered a Greek element in this book. Two of the more noteworthy arguments are by De Vitis and Lewis. De Vitis sees Scobie as a Greek tragic figure. A. A. De Vitis, *Graham Greene* (New York: Twayne Publishers, 1964), pp. 102-103. Lewis analyzes the novel in Aristotelian terms. Lewis, pp. 388-393.

[23]King has a noteworthy Danteian interpretation. Bruce King, "Graham Greene's Inferno," *Etudes Anglaises*, XXI (1968), 35-51.

[24]W. H. Auden, "The Heresy of Our Time," *Graham Greene*, Samuel Hynes, ed. (Englewood Cliffs, Prentice-Hall, Inc., 1973), p. 94.

[25]Graham Greene, *The Heart of the Matter* (New York: The Viking Press, 1948), p. 41.

[26]Kenneth Allott and Miriam Farris, *The Art of Graham Greene* (New York: Russell & Russell, Inc., 1963), p. 224.

[27]Even if, for example, all this seems to be beyond Waugh's compre-

hension. See Waugh, p. 101.

[28]There exists an important letter by Greene in which he says that his "own intention was to make it completely vague as to whether he was expressing his love for the two women or his love for God." Marie-Beatrice Mesnet, *Graham Greene and The Heart of the Matter* (London: Cresset Press, 1954), pp. 103-104.

[29]Graham Greene, *A Sort of Life* (New York: Simon and Schuster, 1971), p. 85.

[30]*Ways of Escape,* p. 123.

[31]*Ibid.,* p. 125.

[32]Prior to the publication of *The End of the Affair* in 1951, Greene had actually tried out the first person narrative approach before, but only in a very limited and rather tentative way—in some short stories and in *The Third Man* (1950), a book which was meant to be read as a screenplay and was not meant to be published as a finished work of fiction.

[33]Charles J. Rolo, "Graham Greene: The Man and the Message," *Atlantic Monthly,* CCVII (May 1961), 65.

[34]Nathan A. Scott, Jr., "Graham Greene: Christian Tragedian," *Graham Greene,* Robert O. Evans, ed. (University of Kentucky Press, 1963), p. 45.

[35]Graham Greene, *The End of the Affair* (London: William Heinemann & Bodley Head, 1974), pp. 99-100.

[36]Karl, p. 90.

[37]Martin Shuttleworth and Simon Raven, "The Art of Fiction: Graham Greene," *Graham Greene,* Samuel Hynes, ed. (Englewood Cliffs: Prentice-Hall, Inc., 1973), p. 161.

[38]Kohn, p. 2.

[39]Shuttleworth and Raven, p. 159.

[40]Paul West, *The Wine of Absurdity* (University Park: The Pennsylvania State University Press, 1966), p. 176.

[41]Lewis, p. 394.

[42]Shuttleworth and Raven, p. 159.

[43]David Pryce-Jones, *Graham Greene* (Edinburgh: Oliver and Boyd, 1970), p. 114.

[44]Herbert R. Haber, "The End of the Catholic Cycle: The Writer Versus the Saint," *Graham Greene,* Robert O. Evans, ed. (University of Kentucky Press, 1963), p. 134.

[45]Pryce-Jones, p. 86.

[46]Frank Kermode, "The House of Fiction: Interviews with Seven English Novelists," *Partisan Review,* XXX (Spring 1963), 67.

[47]*Ibid.*

[48]*A Sort of Life,* p. 167.

[49]Atkins, p. 179.

[50]Sean O'Faolain, "Graham Greene: 'I Suffer, Therefore I Am'," *The Power and the Glory*, R. W. B. Lewis and Peter J. Conn, eds. (New York: The Viking Press, 1970), p. 436.

[51]Francis L. Kunkel, "The Theme of Sin and Grace," *Graham Greene*, Robert O. Evans, ed. (University of Kentucky Press, 1963), p. 51.

[52]Kunkel, *The Labyrinthine Ways of Graham Greene*, p. 20.

[53]Phillips, p. 175.

[54]Pryce-Jones, p. 109.

[55]Morton Dauwen Zabel, "Graham Greene: The Best and the Worst," *The Power and the Glory*, R. W. B. Lewis and Peter J. Conn, eds. (New York: The Viking Press, 1970), p. 368.

[56]Philip Toynbee, "Graham Greene on the Job of the Writer: An Interview," *The Power and the Glory*, R. W. B. Lewis and Peter J. Conn, eds. (New York: The Viking Press, 1970), p. 502.

[57]Between 1951 and 1955, the publication dates of *The End of the Affair* and *The Quiet American*, Greene composed such a wide variety of things that, in retrospect at least, it seems clear he was actually signaling a restless desire for a shift away from the kind of writing which had established his reputation. During those years he published volumes of essays in 1951 and 1953; his first play, entitled *The Living Room*, in 1953; an expanded edition of his previously published short story collection in 1954; and *Loser Takes All*, a comic novelette which he rightly considered to be a frivolity, in 1955. In subsequent years, Greene would return to these modes during periods of creative restlessness. Of these, drama became the favorite because, to him, its social nature provided the greatest means of escape from the sometimes painful experience of writing a novel. It might be noted that although some of his plays did well enough on the stage, none represents a truly major achievements. As for short fiction, during the course of his career Greene has written several stories ("The Basement Room," for example, or "The Destructors") which are of the highest quality. However, there is no denying that his gift for the novel far exceeds that for any other form of creative writing.

[58]David Lodge, "Graham Greene's Comedians," *Commonweal*, LXXXIII (1966), 604-605.

[59]Stanford Sternlicht, "The Sad Comedians: Graham Greene's Later Novels," *Florida Quarterly*, I (1968), 77.

[60]*Ibid.*, p. 65.

IV. *The Quiet American: A Secular Prospect*

[1] Representative of a series of such interpretations is an article by Eric Larsen, "Reconsideration: *The Quiet American,*" *The New Republic* (August 7 & 14, 1976), pp. 40-42.

[2] Two of the most notable exceptions are *The End of the Affair* and *The Human Factor,* but even there Greene attributes to the English settings these qualities to a certain extent.

[3] Philip Stratford, *Faith and Fiction: Creative Process in Greene and Mauriac* (Notre Dame, Indiana: University of Notre Dame Press, 1965), p. 7.

[4] Graham Greene, *The Quiet American* (London: Heinemann, 1960), p. 202.

[5] Gwenn R. Boardman, *Graham Greene: The Aesthetics of Exploration* (Gainesville: University of Florida Press, 1971), p. 36.

[6] *Ibid.*

[7] Arnold P. Hinchliffe, "The Good American," *Twentieth Century,* CLXVIII (December 1960), p. 535.

[8] R. E. Hughes, "*The Quiet American*: The Case Reopened," *Renascence,* XII (Autumn 1959), p. 41.

[9] Stratford, *Faith and Fiction,* p. 309.

[10] Dominguez, a professional aide to Fowler, best represents this ideal synthesis.

[11] Stratford, *Faith and Fiction,* pp. 309-310.

[12] Philip Stratford, ed., *The Portable Graham Greene* (New York: The Viking Press, 1973), p. vii.

[13] *Ibid.,* pp. vii-viii.

[14] David Pryce-Jones, *Graham Greene* (Edinburgh: Oliver and Boyd, 1970), p. 93.

[15] Francis L. Kunkel, *The Labyrinthine Ways of Graham Greene* (New York: Sheed and Ward, 1959), p. 148.

[16] Boardman, p. 109.

[17] *Ibid.,* p. 108.

[18] See, for example, the argument of Hughes, pp. 42, 49.

[19] Stratford, *The Portable Graham Greene,* p. 582.

[20] Kenneth Allott and Miriam Farris, *The Art of Graham Greene* (New York: Russell & Russell, Inc., 1963), p. 163.

[21] A. A. DeVitis, *Graham Greene* (New York: Twayne Publishers, 1964), p. 117.

[22] Frederick R. Karl, *The Contemporary English Novel* (New York: Farrar, Straus and Giroux, 1965), p. 93.

[23] Boardman, pp. 116-117.

V. Comic Directions

[1] Graham Greene, *Our Man in Havana* (London: William Heinemann & Bodley Head, 1977), p. 242.

[2] Anony., "Mr. Greene Entertains," *The Times Literary Supplement* (October 10, 1958), p. 573.

[3] In thinking back to how he came to "discover comedy" during "the course of the blackest book" he has written, Greene indicates that, even before *The Quiet American* and *Our Man in Havana*, he had been drifting toward the "tragicomic region" and that the short story "A Visit to Morin" (published in the 1963 volume of short stories, *A Sense of Reality*, a volume which incidentally contains some of Greene's finest short stories) essentially anticipates *A Burnt-Out Case*. *Ways of Escape*, pp. 266-267.

[4] Graham Greene, *A Burnt-Out Case* (William Heinemann & Bodley Head, 1974), p. 230.

[5] The following, then, is more than just a repetition of the references made to *Journey Without Maps* in the introductory chapter.

[6] *Journey Without Maps*, p. 11.

[7] *Ibid.*, p. 277.

[8] Carolyn D. Scott, "The Witch at the Corner: Notes on Graham Greene's Mythology," *Graham Greene*, Robert O. Evans, ed. (University of Kentucky Press, 1963), p. 243.

[9] This situation may recall the one found in *Victory*, and thus seems to imply that although Greene reached a point much earlier in his career when he consciously fought against the influence of Joseph Conrad, he could still feel the powerful pull of one of his original mentors.

[10] A. A. DeVitis, *Graham Greene* (New York: Twayne Publishers, 1964), p. 121.

[11] Gwenn R. Boardman, *Graham Greene: The Aesthetics of Exploration* (Gainesville: University of Florida Press, 1971), p. 141.

[12] The most conspicuous of these readers was Evelyn Waugh. See *Ways of Escape*, pp. 263-264.

[13] Muller notes that Colin's philosophy is similar to that of Pierre Teilhard de Chardin described in the latter's *The Phenomenon of Man*, a book Greene has admitted had some influence on the writing of *A Burnt-Out Case*. C. H. Muller, "Graham Greene and the Absurd," *UNISA English Studies*, X (June 1972), p. 34.

[14] In having Querry make this warning, Greene obviously was also thinking of his critics. But, predictably, this allegorical story, because it has certain parallels with Greene's career, has drawn such conclusions as Kermode's that Querry, "the famous Catholic architect, is a famous Catholic writer thinly disguised. . . ." Frank Kermode, "Mr. Greene's Eggs and

Crosses," *Encounter,* XVI (April 1961), 71. Boardman is closer to the truth when she suggests that "it would be foolish to draw an oversimplified meaning from Querry's parable" because the story "is describing a universal malady, not Greene's personal spiritual anguish." Boardman, p. 156.

[15] David Pryce-Jones, *Graham Greene* (Edinburgh: Oliver and Boyd, 1970), p. 96.

[16] James Noxon, "Kierkegaard's Stages and *A Burnt-Out Case,*" *Review of English Literature,* III (January 1962), 90-101. Also see Boardman, p. 142.

[17] Boardman, p. 142.

[18] Gene D. Phillips, "Graham Greene: On the Screen," *Graham Greene,* Samuel Hynes, ed. (Englewood Cliffs: Prentice-Hall, Inc., 1973), p. 174.

[19] *Ibid.*

[20] If this hasn't become the only recognized reading, it's probably due to what might be considered the novel's only real flaw. In his previous novels, Greene had always tried, and mostly succeeded, in creating protagonists whom he depicted both with objectivity and emotional sympathy. In this book, the scale occasionally tips too much toward overtly sympathetic identification with Querry. This might have been perceived as simply another fictional strategy were it not for an added factor. Greene invests so many personal details in Querry that it's sometimes inescapable to conclude this characters acts as Greene's alter-ego. In this regard, a number of the book's reviewers noted that between Querry and Greene there were quite a few significant parallels, so many in fact that it's tempting at times to read the story as a kind of autobiographical confession. Obviously, this wasn't Greene's intention. But because it's possible to make a reasonably good case for such an interpretation, and because several reviewers who chose to give the story such a reading were highly influential, this reading of *A Burnt-Out Case* persists to this day.

[21] Graham Greene, *In Search of a Character* (New York: The Viking Press, 1962), p. xiii.

[22] *A Burnt-Out Case* comes in a close third. But it should be emphasized that this problem springs up from the fact so many of its readers rather willfully choose to read it as a kind of autobiographical confession rather than from Greene's strategic use of ambiguity.

[23] Lodge argues that Greene's fiction has entered a world "in which the eternal verities are obscured" to the point where life becomes a black comedy and that hence the only "recourse is to play in this comedy, as Brown does." David Lodge, "Graham Greene's Comedians," *Commonweal,* LXXXIII (1966), 605. But it will be shown that "the eternal verities" are very much alive in the world of this novel and that Brown does not remain

merely a desperate comedian.

[24]Phillips, p. 174.

[25]Muller, p. 38.

[26]DeVitis is correct in pointing out that the book is an unusual comedy, but he goes too far when he concludes that "there is movement only from horror to despair." A. A. DeVitis, "Greene's *The Comedians*: Hollower Men," *Renascence,* XVIII (1966), 129. The evidence that will be presented will show that if Brown's life does not move toward a "happy ending," it does move toward an affirmative one.

[27]Graham Greene, *The Comedians* (New York: The Viking Press, 1966), p. 215.

[28]Her red hair, her black lover, her acceptance of everything, including death, as "fun" coincide with what we find out about Aunt Augusta in *Travels With My Aunt.* Here is one illustration of Greene's habit of introducing a minor character in one book and then developing him in the following as a major character. This is one of the elements giving the canon of Greene's works the quality of a chronicle.

[29]In Jones' bifurcated political world, there are the "tarts" and the "toffs." As he says, the "toffs can do without the tarts, but the tarts can't do without the toffs" because the toffs are the ones of material substance (*C,* p. 18).

[30]Muller, p. 44.

[31]Stanford Sternlicht, "The Sad Comedies: Graham Greene's Later Novels," *Florida Quarterly,* I (1968), p. 76.

[32]In a sermon near the end of the novel a young priest, obviously meant to represent the increasing militancy of a part of the modern Catholic church, says that even violence may be a form of love. Once again, by the way, it appears that this minor character grew in the imagination of Greene until in *The Honorary Consul* he became a major figure.

[33]It might be noted that Greene has thought of himself as a kind of manic-depressive, and that during this period he felt the manic side prevailing. *Ways of Escape,* p. 296.

[34]*Ways of Escape,* p. 285.

[35]Haskel Frankel, "Fiction: *Travels With My Aunt,*" *Saturday Review* (January 24, 1970), p. 38.

[36]*Ways of Escape,* pp. 296-297.

[37]Graham Greene, *Travels With My Aunt* (New York: The Viking Press, 1969), p. 10.

[38]In the course of *Travels With My Aunt,* it becomes clear that Greene takes us to revisit many of the old places and ideas which he has frequented in his former books. In the process he reminds us where he has been, yet at the same time he manages to suggest where he still might be

going, so that it's much too simple to refer to the book, as one critic has done, as "the comical resume of his entire career. . . ." Anon., "Graham Greene: The Man Within," *Graham Greene,* Samuel Hynes, ed. (Englewood Cliffs: Prentice-Hall, Inc., 1973), p. 13.

[39] Jack Newcombe, "Greene, 'The Funny Writer,' on Comedy," *Life,* 68 (January 23, 1970), p. 10.

[40] That the novel ends with some of Browning's more platitudinous words—"God's in his heaven/All's right with the world!"—calls for some explanation. Such an ending might strike one at first as being so glib and hackneyed that one is prone to think Greene is surely being ironic. After all, Greene is not likely to end a novel on a note of easy piety since he has mocked false sentiment all of his life. And then one recalls a famous remark made by O'Faolain to the effect that Greene is a writer who is pleased to reverse the lines of Browning to read "God's in his heaven, all's wrong with the world." Sean O'Faolain, "Graham Greene: 'I Suffer, Therefore I Am',' *The Power and the Glory,* R. W. B. Lewis and Peter J. Conn, eds. (New York: The Viking Press, 1970), p. 434. Thus one is bound to suspect that Greene is certainly having a great deal of personal fun with these lines. However, once one has sifted through the various possible interpretations of Greene's ambiguous ending, the most obvious comes back to mind. Clearly, Greene would not employ Browning's lines to the extent of ironically over-turning the whole novel. The reason why these lines, then, form the proper final note is because they can express the understanding at which Henry has arrived—that what we do find in our quasi-secular world is worthy of celebration after all.

VI. *The Late Novels*

[1] The fact that not long thereafter Greene came out with the first volume of his autobiography (*A Sort of Life*) seemed to add weight to this assumption for a while.

[2] Graham Greene, *The Honorary Consul* (New York: Simon and Schuster, 1973), pp. 218-219.

[3] Any number of reviews and articles might be cited. But the way Timothy Foote's review of *The Honorary Consul* begins is especially reveal-ing of this view of Greene's writing. The first sentence of this review reads: "The Hound of Heaven is still hell-bent in pursuit of Graham Greene." Timothy Foote, "Our Man in Gehenna," *Time,* Vol. 102 (September 17, 1973), p. 99.

[4] *In Search of a Character* (New York: The Viking Press, 1962),

p. 13.

[5]Robert Osterman, "Interview with Graham Greene," *Catholic World*, CLXX (February 1950), p. 360.

[6]Anony., "New Honor and New Novel," *Life,* LX (February 4, 1966), p. 44.

[7]*Ways of Escape,* p. 306.

[8]This is a process which, by Greene's own admission, his novels often undergo, especially with reference to character development.

[9]Because of these elements, especially that of violence, Greene has stated he was "more than usually dissatisfied" with this novel, so much so, in fact, that he seriously considered not publishing it. *Ways of Escape,* p. 309.

[10]The fact that Castle lives in Berkhamsted, the birthplace of Greene, is the most prominent sign that Greene has identified perhaps more closely with this character than with any of his other protagonists.

[11]Graham Greene, *The Human Factor* (New York: Simon and Schuster, 1978), p. 52.

[12]Clive James, "Birthmarks, Chess Games and Wise Policemen," *New Statesman,* Vol. 85 (17 March 1978), p. 359.

[13]Walter Sullivan, "Documents from the Ice Age: Recent British Novels," *The Sewanee Review,* Vol. 86 (Spring 1978), p. 323.

[14]Because of its thematic complexity, *Doctor Fischer of Geneva* is destined to become one of Greene's most controversial and perhaps most misunderstood books. Already, the reactions to it vary from the curtest dismissal (It's called Greene's "slightest, his most melodramatic, and his most sentimental" book in: "Briefly Noted," *New Yorker,* Vol. 56, June 2, 1980, p. 138) to the highest praise (Walter Clemons concludes that it's simply "perfect" in: "Frozen in Greeneland," *Newsweek,* May 19, 1980, p. 91).

[15]Graham Greene, *Doctor Fischer of Geneva, or the Bomb Party* (New York: Simon and Schuster, 1980), pp. 71-72.

[16]Graham Greene, *Monsignor Quixote* (New York: Simon and Schuster, 1982), p. 221.

[17]See, for example, the recent essay by Maria Couto, "On the road," *New Statesman* (September 17, 1982), p. 22.

VII. A Look at the Final Achievement

[1]As late as in the fall of 1982, for instance, Greene indicated a plan to write a full-length memoir of the late Torrijos Herrera, Panama's political

leader for many years. See: J. D. Reed, "The Surprise of Spiritual Slap-stick," *Time* (September 20, 1982), p. 75.

[2] The reference is to such writers as Angus Wilson, Anthony Powell, Alan Sillitoe, Margaret Drabble, John Fowles, and V. S. Naipaul.

[3] Greene is especially remindful of Hardy, Lawrence, and Conrad in this regard.

X.
SELECTED BIBLIOGRAPHY

Allott, Kenneth and Miriam Farris. *The Art of Graham Greene.* New York: Russell & Russell, 1963.

Atkins, John. *Graham Greene: A Biographical and Literary Study.* London: J. Calder, 1957.

Bell, Pearl K. "Aging Novelists," *Commentary,* Vol. 70 (September 1980), 70-73.

Bergonzi, Bernard. "Conspicuous Absentee," *Encounter,* Vol. 55 (August/ September 1980), 44, 46-48, 50, 52-56.

Boardman, Gwenn R. *Graham Greene: The Aesthetics of Exploration.* Gainesville: University of Florida Press, 1971.

Burgess, Anthony. "A Talk with Graham Greene," *Saturday Review* (May 1982), 44-47.

—. "Travels with Graham Greene," *Saturday Review* (January 1981), 64-65.

Clemons, Walter. "Frozen in Greeneland," *Newsweek* (May 19, 1980), 91-92.

DeVitis, A. A. "Greene's *The Comedians*: Hollower Men," *Renascence.* XVIII (1966), 129-136, 146.

—. *Graham Greene.* New York: Twayne Publishers, 1964.

Donoghue, Denis. "A Novel of Thought, Action and Pity," *The New York Times Book Review* (February 26, 1978), 1, 43.

Ellis, William D. "The Grand Theme of Graham Greene," *Southwest Re-*

view, XLI (Summer 1956), 239-250.

Emerson, Gloria. "Our Man in Antibes," *Rolling Stone* (March 9, 1978), 45-49.

Evans, R. O., ed. *Graham Greene: Some Critical Considerations.* Lexington, Kentucky: University of Kentucky Press, 1963.

Frankel, Haskel. "Fiction: *Travels With My Aunt,*" *Saturday Review* (January 24, 1970), 38.

Greene, Graham. *Another Mexico.* New York: The Viking Press, 1967.

—. *Brighton Rock.* London: Heinemann & Bodley Head, 1975.

—. *A Burnt-Out Case.* London: Heinemann & Bodley Head, 1974.

—. *Collected Essays.* New York: Viking, 1969.

—. *The Comedians.* New York: Viking, 1966.

—. *The Confidential Agent.* London: Heinemann & Bodley Head, 1971.

—. *Doctor Fischer of Geneva, or the Bomb Party.* New York: Simon and Schuster, 1980.

—. *The End of the Affair.* London: Heinemann & Bodley Head, 1974.

—. *England Made Me.* London: Heinemann & Bodley Head, 1970.

—. *A Gun for Sale.* London: Heinemann & Bodley Head, 1973.

—. *The Heart of the Matter.* New York: Viking, 1948.

—. *The Honorary Consul.* New York: Simon and Schuster, 1973.

—. *The Human Factor.* New York: Simon and Schuster, 1978.

—. *In Search of a Character: Two African Journals.* New York: Viking, 1962.

—. *It's a Battlefield.* London: Heinemann & Bodley Head, 1975.

—. *Journey Without Maps.* New York: Viking, 1965.

—. *The Man Within.* London: Heinemann & Bodley Head, 1976.

—. *The Ministry of Fear.* London: Heinemann, 1956.

—. *Monsignor Quixote.* New York: Simon and Schuster, 1982.

—. *Our Man in Havana.* London: Heinemann & Bodley Head, 1977.

—. *The Pleasure Dome.* London: Secker & Warburg, 1972.

—. *The Power and the Glory.* London: Heinemann & Bodley Head, 1979.

—. *The Quiet American.* London: Heinemann, 1955.

—. *A Sort of Life.* New York: Simon and Schuster, 1971.

—. *Stamboul Train.* London: Heinemann & Bodley Head, 1974.

—. *Travels With My Aunt.* New York: Viking, 1970.

—. *Ways of Escape.* New York: Simon and Schuster, 1980.

Hinchliffe, A. P. "The Good American," *Twentieth Century,* CLXVIII (December, 1960), 529-539.

Hughes, R. E. "The Quiet American: The Case Reopened," *Renascence,* XII (Autumn 1959), 41-42, 49.

Hynes, Samuel, ed. *Graham Greene.* Englewood Cliffs: Prentice-Hall, Inc., 1973.

James, Clive. "Birthmarks, Chess Games and Wise Policemen," *New Statesman,* Vol. 85 (March 17, 1978), 359-360.

Karl, F. R. "Graham Greene's Demoniacal Heroes." In *The Contemporary English Novel.* New York: Farrar, Straus, & Company, 1962.

Kermode, Frank. "The House of Fiction: Interviews with Seven English Novelists," *Partisan Review,* XXX (Spring 1963), 61-82.

—. "Mr. Greene's Eggs and Crosses," *Encounter,* XVI (April 1961), 69-75.

King, Bruce. "Graham Greene's Inferno," *Etudes Anglaises,* XXI (1968), 35-51.

Kohn, Lynette. *Graham Greene: The Major Novels.* Palo Alto: Stanford Honors Essays in Humanities, no. IV, 1961.

Kunkel, F. L. *The Labyrinthine Ways of Graham Greene.* New York: Sheed and Ward, 1959.

Lehmann, J. "The Blundering, Ineffectual American," *New Republic,* CXXXIV (March 12, 1956), 26-27.

Lewis, R. W. B. and Peter J. Conn, eds. *The Power and the Glory.* New York: The Viking Press, 1970.

Lodge, David. "Graham Greene's Comedians," *Commonweal,* LXXXIII (1966), 604-606.

—. "Graham Greene." In *Six Contemporary British Novelists.* George Stade, ed. New York: Columbia University Press, 1976.

Mesnet, Marie-Beatrice. *Graham Greene and the Heart of the Matter.* London: Cresset Press, 1954.

Muller, C. H. "Graham Greene and the Absurd," *UNISA English Studies,* X (June 1972), 34-45.

Newcombe, Jack. "Greene, 'The Funny Writer,' On Comedy," *Life,* 68 (January 23, 1970), 10.

Noxon, James. "Kierkegaard's Stages and *A Burnt-Out Case,*" *Review of English Literature,* III (January 1962), 90-101.

Osterman, Robert. "Interview with Graham Greene," *Catholic World,* CLXX (February 1950), 356-361.

Pritchett, V. S. "The Human Factor in Graham Greene," *The New York Times Magazine* (February 26, 1978), 33-36, 38, 40-42, 44, 46.

Pryce-Jones, David. *Graham Greene.* Edinburgh: Oliver and Boyd, 1970.

Redman, Ben Ray. "Chance Acquaintances," *The Saturday Review of Literature* (March 18, 1933), 489.

Rolo, Charles J. "Graham Greene: The Man and the Message," *Atlantic Monthly*, CCVII (May 1961), 60-65.

Smith, A. J. M. "Graham Greene's Theological Thrillers," *Queen's Quarterly*, LXVIII (Spring 1961), 15-33.

Sternlicht, Sanford. "The Sad Comedies: Graham Greene's Later Novels," *Florida Quarterly*, I (1968), 65-77.

Stone, Robert. "Gin and Nostalgia," *Harper's* (April 1978), 79-80, 83.

Stratford, Philip. *Faith and Fiction: Creative Process in Greene and Mauriac.* Notre Dame: University of Notre Dame Press, 1964.

—, ed. *The Portable Graham Greene.* New York: The Viking Press, 1973.

Sullivan, Walter. "Documents from the Ice Age: Recent British Novels," *The Sewanee Review*, Vol. 86 (Spring 1978), 320-325.

Unsigned. "New Honor and New Novel," *Life,* 60 (February 4, 1966), 43-44.

—. "When Greene is Red," *Newsweek*, XLVII (October 1, 1956), 10.

West, Paul. "Graham Greene." In *The Wine of Absurdity.* University Park: Pennsylvania State University Press, 1966.

Wolf, Peter. *Graham Greene the Entertainer.* Carbondale, Illinois: Southern Illinois University Press, 1972.

Wood, Michael. "Spies Together," *Saturday Review*, Vol. 5 (April 1, 1978), 33-34.

Zabel, Morton Dauwen. "Graham Greene," *The Nation,* Vol. 157 (July 3, 1943), 18-20.

XI.
INDEX

DATE DUE

DE 31 '97	